UNLEASH THE POWER OF YOUR MIND!

UNLEASH THE POWER OF YOUR MIND!

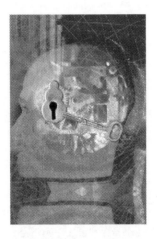

REACH YOUR TRUE POTENTIAL

Estelle Gibbins

BA (Psych), Dip Health Science, NLP Practitioner

BALBOA
PRESS

A DIVISION OF HAY HOUSE

Balboa Press books may be ordered through booksellers or by contacting:

Balboa Press
A Division of Hay House
1663 Liberty Drive
Bloomington, IN 47403
www.balboapress.com.au
1-(877) 407-4847

ISBN: 978-1-4525-0753-8 (sc)
ISBN: 978-1-4525-0754-5 (e)

Printed in the United States of America

Balboa Press rev. date: 10/16/2012

CONTENTS

DEDICATION

For the seemingly endless support from my beloved family—Mum, Dad (no longer with us, and yet always here in spirit), brother Simon, sister Gretta. Without your help and encouragement, I would be but a shadow of myself.

And for my gorgeous son, Ethan—you are, quite simply, the light of my life. I count every day that I get to spend in your company, as a magic gift.

Thanks to all those who have helped me in my life journey, through experiences good and not so good . . . you have all added so much color and joy to the fabric that is my life.

Thanks go too to the authors, mentors and coaches that have helped me along the way . . . Bob Proctor, John Assaraf, Louise Hay, Jack Canfield, Peggy McColl, Sonia Choquette, Esther and Jerry Hicks, Dr Wayne Dyer, Lilou Mace, Tim Ferriss, Paul McKenna, John Demartini, Lynn Grabhorn, Anthony Robbins, Christopher Howard, Richard Bach, Marianne Williamson, Joe Vitale, Neville Goddard, and Robin Sharma.

I love how we are all a "work in progress" and knowing that the teacher will arrive when the student is ready is a wonderful feeling.

EPIGRAPH

"Tell me how you think, and I will tell you what kind of a person you are.
Tell me how you think, and I will tell you how rich you will be.
Tell me how you think, and I will tell you what level of education
and the degree of higher learning you have obtained and will obtain.
Tell me how you think, and I will tell you
how much mental and spiritual peace you possess.
Tell me how you think, and I will tell you what the future holds for you.
Tell me what you think, and I will tell you
how many friends and how many enemies you have.
Tell me what you think, and I will tell you what others think of you.
Tell me what you think, and I will tell you how healthy you are.
Indeed, your life is shaped by the quality of your individual thoughts.
A person's quality of life is determined by the quality of
his each and every thought."

~ Source Unknown ~

PREFACE

The aim of this book is to create a comprehensive, easy to understand, useful tool to:

- Help people understand how to use their natural mind power more effectively;
- To show people how to manifest their dreams into reality quickly and easily; and
- Help people reach their true potential.

The end result is that I want people to receive better results in any area of their life that they have the desire to do so.

You can view this book as an owner's manual for the mind, in that it explains how to more fully utilize your innate mind power to assist you to succeed in all areas of your life. It is not my intention to tell you HOW to think, while you work or play. I don't intend to tell you HOW to do tasks that are specific to your particular occupation, sport or role in life. This book is about how to 'run' your mind more efficiently and effectively, and it is my intention to share with you many simple exercises that will enable you to get the most out of what you already have—and thus receive more remarkable results in any and every aspect of your life.

With all of the scientific and technological advancements that are occurring on a minute-by-minute basis in this 21st century, I began to wonder why so many people still see themselves as unhappy and lacking in self confidence in their day-to-day lives. It seems to be a 'modern day affliction', this sense of unrest and lack of fulfillment. Instead of living peacefully in this age of plenty, many people are feeling more and more empty inside.

From my perspective, this is ironic, given the mind-blowing potential that exists in side of us, from the moment of our birth. For a number of years, it has been generally agreed that we use less than 1% of our natural brain power, but research is now indicating that that figure is closer to 1000% or even less! Now that means that we have barely even scratched the surface of our mind-boggling brain capacity.

Before you start to argue or panic, I want to assure you that this book is NOT about Mind Control. It's about enhancing our ability to access our mental skills and abilities, when we choose to do so. At it's core, this book is simply a lesson in unleashing our natural abilities, and getting out of our own way, so we can achieve more of what is possible for us in all areas of our life. To achieve these results, we need to look more towards accessing and more fully utilizing our subconscious mental abilities.

Our subconscious mind is in charge of our entire destiny and controls each and every aspect of our existence. It shapes our emotions, beliefs, and self-confidence, our whole identity. Now if we are able to communicate with this awesome power source, to understand how it works and to subsequently re-program it to operate more efficiently, it stands to reason that we could become a "whole new person"—able to overcome all the obstacles of life, experience transformation and rebirth, and live the best life possible.

On a practical level, what does this mean? It means fully utilizing all of our innate skills—using what we have been born with to the best of our ability. It doesn't require buying into the latest trend, whether that be gadgets, books, courses etc. That's not to say some books, courses, programs or gadgets won't be useful on your quest to live to your truest potential—they may well be. But my focus here is to guide you to tap into your INNATE abilities, and on developing your natural "hardware" so that you can flourish into the best possible person you can be. Now that's a goal worth striving for!

CHAPTER 1

UNDERSTAND YOUR BRAIN

The subconscious mind is an amazing part of our human existence which essentially controls our whole existence by shaping our behavior, identity, and beliefs. It allows us to form relationships with other people to fulfill our dreams and goals, allowing us to create whatever we desire. Although the exact scope and abilities of the subconscious mind have not yet been discovered, I believe that by harnessing this unique thinking system, we can create an amazing life and achieve true happiness. Everything begins with a single thought, which is the primary signal that enters our subconscious minds. Our thoughts are what guide and command the subconscious mind. This means that essentially, a person's entire world is shaped by his or her thoughts and that every single thought has a consequence.

"Every thought of yours is a real thing—a force"
~ Prentice Mulford ~

A beautiful and positive thought has the potential to create a whole new story in one's life. At a basic, fundamental level, whatever we think, we create. Our existence is all about thoughts, which all lead to creation; so it follows that if you think something repeatedly, you will eventually create that in your life. Whatever reality people create begins as a simple thought in their head. A person's life is the result of his or her every single thought. What separates individuals from one another are the kinds of thoughts they have. So it can be said that the major difference between a successful person and one who has failed could be identified as the difference in their beliefs and the thought system by which they operate. Poverty and failure are the result of poor thoughts, while wealth and success are the result of rich thoughts. You ARE what you believe. It doesn't matter whether you think that you will succeed or think that you will fail; in both cases you've thought accurately. If you think you will succeed, your positive thoughts will move and guide you toward success. If, from the very beginning, you think that you will fail, your negative thoughts will generate negative feelings in your body, and as a result, you will either give up or your behavior and actions will CAUSE you to fail. Your thoughts are POWERFUL and can bring about health, just as easily as they can cause illness. People who have beautiful and hopeful thoughts stay healthy. People who have negative and cynical thoughts not only face failure in life, but they also attract health problems.

Your mind is like a factory; it is responsible for generating your thoughts at every moment. On average, each human conceives about sixty-thousand thoughts a day, and these thoughts are what shapes one's life. Thoughts take form in the world as created realities. Thoughts can transform into wealth; and a thought can even bring peace of mind or, alternatively, it can lead to the experience of anxiety and depression. Thoughts generate self-confidence and self-esteem. Thoughts are what induce either feelings of love or feelings of hatred. Thoughts either create friendships or enemies. Thoughts produce either happiness or sorrow. Ultimately, thoughts bring about either success or failure.

"Whatever the mind can conceive, it can achieve."
~ W.Clement Stone ~

THE DIFFERENCE BETWEEN THE CONSCIOUS & THE SUBCONSCIOUS MINDS

The conscious and the subconscious minds are merely two separate spheres of activity within your brain. Your conscious mind is the rational or logical mind, whereas your subconscious mind is the 'automatic' part of the brain than operates below the level of your conscious awareness. Without any conscious choice on your part, your heart keeps pumping blood, your blood vessels expand and contract as your blood pressure changes according to the activities the body is engaged in and the emotions you experience. These are just two examples of the multitude of functions that may seem as if they 'just happen', but are actually the result of your subconscious mental processes, hard at work. Most people are not aware that they even have a subconscious mind, although they access it multiple times each day just to survive.

Your subconscious mind is very powerful and makes up a great percentage of your mental processes, even though you are unaware of it. Your subconscious mind is easily impressed upon by the thoughts and mental focus of the conscious mind. Your subconscious does not reason—it simply reacts to and follows the instructions and guidance of the conscious mind. Your subconscious can be described as a bed of soil that accepts any kind of seed, whether good or bad. Your mental thoughts are active; they are seeds in the garden of your subconscious mind. Negative, destructive thoughts that may be the result of long term anxiety or depression, continue to work negatively in your subconscious. Sooner or later, these thoughts surface to take shape as an outer experience that corresponds with or mirrors their content. Therefore the old saying, "Be careful what you wish for," actually has some firm foundation in modern psychology.

The focus of this book is maximizing human potential by learning simple skills to better utilize the amazing powerhouse that is the subconscious mind. First though, we need to understand exactly what is the subconscious mind. And this is not a simple question to answer!

FUNCTIONS OF THE SUBCONSCIOUS MIND

To fully understand the many functions of the subconscious mind, lets take a quick look at some of the roles that the Subconscious Mind plays in our lives.

The subconscious mind will do whatever we ask it to do. It is an amazing servant to us. There are no limits to what our subconscious mind will do for us, in fact it is only limited by the restrictions we place upon it (and ourselves) through the beliefs we have created during our lives. If we have a belief that it's not likely that we'll ever be rich, our subconscious will do everything in its power to see that our belief comes true for us. The subconscious mind does not discriminate when it comes to thoughts and feelings; it responds to fearful thoughts as well as loving thoughts. The subconscious responds to every desire and imaginative thought we choose to entertain. So, achieving and maintaining some degree of awareness of our thoughts (since the subconscious hears every thought and responds accordingly) is certainly a skill worth having and honing. Our subconscious mind is our friend and is always there for us and it never judges any of our thoughts, feelings or actions. Remember, our subconscious is the non-critical, non-analytical aspect of our mind—though we often judge ourselves with our conscious mind, according to the belief systems we have created for ourselves. As our good friend and ally, our subconscious mind is also extraordinarily protective of us. It will repress painful memories until we are ready and willing to heal them.

The realm of the subconscious is where our heart lies. The spectrum of emotions from love through to fear are recorded and stored within the subconscious realm. Our subconscious memorizes all our feelings about every event we experience and encodes these memories in the cellular structure of our bodies. So, whenever a familiar event occurs, the feelings we have developed from earlier similar events are felt and then stored instantaneously in the cells of our body. Also, the thoughts and beliefs we have created regarding those "similar events" also show up instantly. Our subconscious brings our thoughts and feelings to us instantly and automatically as each event in our life occurs. Now, because the subconscious is the realm of the heart, it easily overrides the rational thoughts from our conscious mind whenever a conflict arises. Let's take a look at exactly how our subconscious mind wins the majority of these battles with our conscious mind.

Suppose a person (let's call her Jane) makes a "conscious" decision to lose weight. But one day at the office, someone offers Jane a chocolate croissant. Now, let's say Jane holds a belief in her conscious mind that chocolate croissants are fattening—though she absolutely LOVES croissants. Jane eyes the croissant longingly, but tells herself that croissants are definitely fattening and certainly cannot be found anywhere on her carefully constructed list of edibles for her diet. Not a problem. Because, you see, Jane has willpower. And fortitude. And she's sticking to her diet. She'll just pass on this one, no matter how good it looks. Besides, if she wants to lose weight, passing on the croissant is the rational, logical thing to do. And Jane's conscious mind knows that this is what's best for her. Right? But, as if the world has somehow conspired against her, the beautiful, wondrous aroma arising from the croissant reaches her nostrils; and, making matters worse, Barbara from accounting, a notorious pastry lover, is crossing the room eyeing Jane's croissant! Without hesitation, Jane snatches the croissant and profusely thanks her thoughtful coworker. She eats the croissant and with each bite, Jane feels the accompanying sting of guilt from having cheated on her diet.

How did this happen? Pretty simple. The strength of Jane's emotional desire to eat the chocolate treat was greater than her desire to lose weight. In order to stop eating pastries, Jane would have to strengthen her desire—at the subconscious level—to lose weight, so that her desire to lose weight would become stronger than her desire to eat chocolate croissants. The emotional strength of our love (or fear) held in our subconscious minds will almost ALWAYS override any rational thoughts coming from our conscious minds. When it comes to a battle of the minds, the subconscious mind will almost always win out.

THE KEY TO EXPERIENCING SUCCESS IN CREATING WHAT WE DESIRE, IS TO CONVINCE OUR SUB-CONSCIOUS MIND TO GO ALONG WITH THE DECISIONS OUR CONSCIOUS MIND MAKES!

Situated deep within the subconscious is the creative, imaginative part of our mind. And the power of this imagination process is LIMITLESS! Anything we can conceive or imagine can come into being. Imagination is the seed of genius, and these seeds of genius are readily available to everyone. All great artists, thinkers, and inventors learn to utilize their imaginative powers within the subconscious. Of course, there is, as always, another side to the coin. When we allow our imagination to be ruled by FEAR, disastrous results can occur—because what we imagine DOES come into being. Our subconscious does not discriminate. But it does its best to create what we picture or imagine. It will work just as hard for us to create the negative imagery we present to it as well as the positive imagery, because the imagination can be used in any fashion we decree. The good news is our benevolent subconscious is always ready and willing to follow our instructions. And we can always change the ways in which we use our imagination. We can choose to cultivate our imagination to create what is always in our highest good.

Our subconscious mind records all of the events that occur within the field of our awareness; all thoughts and feelings about those events; all memories; and it makes a record of all the meanings our conscious mind assigns to those events. The meanings we give to our experiences in life make up our belief systems. So it stands to reason that the subconscious stores our belief systems, organizes them, and brings them to forward into our conscious awareness when they need to access them in any relevant situation or event. Our subconscious mind has a library filled with ALL our thoughts; feelings; memories; and belief systems from our life experiences—all neatly categorized. And any time, when we choose to become still and self-aware, we can access any part of our library. Our subconscious will retrieve any memory we choose to recall. If we desire to discover or remember an event that is at the core of one of our belief systems, all we need do is become quiet in our mind, ask clearly, and our mental 'Librarian' can easily locate anything within the vast library of our mind.

All our thoughts and feelings have an amazing creative ability, so when we make the effort to be still and access our subconscious mind, we can inform our subconscious (through our thoughts, feelings and imagination) what our desires are regarding any particular thing, event or experience. And in turn, our subconscious informs our Soul, or Higher Self, of our desires. This creative process is always occurring regardless of what our dominant state of mind might be at a given point. But the optimal state of mind in which the creative process has the greatest potential for success is the state of mind in which alpha and/or theta states are dominant, for it is in this quiet, prayerful or hypnotic state of mind that the different parts of our mind (Conscious, Subconscious and Higher Self) are present and highly focused.

Our amazing subconscious is also an incredible editor who happens to be available 24 hours a day, 7 days a week, 365 days per year. Our subconscious mind never sleeps, so whenever we decide to change our mind about who we are, our subconscious mind is at our service. All that is required is desire, commitment, and silence. You could say that we are the authors of countless books about who we are, and that these books are stored in the wonderful library of our subconscious. Given that we are the initial authors of these works of art, it is often forgotten that we also have the power to rewrite these books at any time we choose.

Human beings are a matrix of energy. We are a field of energy that reflects our state of consciousness in every moment in time. The subconscious directs our energy, generating and emitting energy relentlessly. We can be happy; peaceful; joyful; angry; hateful; loving; creative; lazy; hyper; and on and on. The matrix of energy we choose to be at any point in time also draws to us matching fields of energy. Loving energy attracts loving energy. Fearful energy attracts fearful energy. We draw people and events to us based on the energy we emit; and this energy is based on our state of consciousness. Current popular psychology labels this phenomenon as the Law of Attraction. Since our state of consciousness is a reflection of our belief systems, which, in turn is a reflection of our collected thoughts and feelings; we must change our thoughts and feelings—and thus, our beliefs—if we want to change our energy.

Our powerful subconscious automatically performs for us all of the habitual behavior to run our mind and body. We don't even have to think about the way we sit or walk or stand. It's all automatic. We have trained our subconscious well. We have even trained our subconscious to drive our cars for us while we daydream. Have you ever reached the end of a car journey and paused to wonder how you got from point A to point B? Have you ever found yourself suddenly asking, "Who's been driving the car for the last ten minutes?" because you've been off somewhere fantasizing? The subconscious will learn and carry out any automatic behavior we choose to teach it, although teaching it to drive our car while we daydream may not be the wisest thing to do! Our subconscious also automates our reactions to simple day-to-day events including our interactions with people. How many times have you responded automatically when you were being introduced to a new acquaintance, only to realize that they didn't even ask the question that you expected or answered? A little embarrassing, isn't it?

We all have automatic reactions to politicians from different political parties that we are probably totally unaware of. Most of our "reactions" to politicians come from our programming. Our reactions might be simply based on a politician's membership in a political party we don't see eye to eye with, or they could be based on the beliefs or policies a specific politician espouses. But our reaction, favorable or unfavorable, is generally automatic. It is the same with our responses to many of the people in our lives. When we see a friend or loved one, the feeling that automatically arises in the cells of our body is usually a good feeling—we may even smile. When we see someone we have difficulty getting along with, the feelings aren't always so good. But what's important to understand is that these feelings arise AUTOMATICALLY. We don't really think about having the feelings, they arise instantaneously. They are experienced automatically because the vast majority of us are living our daily lives on auto-pilot, and our subconscious is simply carrying out our pre-programmed reactions to the events life presents to us.

Our magical subconscious regulates all involuntary functions of the body. The subconscious mind breathes for us; circulates the blood throughout our body; heals us when we are sick or injured; and is in charge of digestion and elimination of waste products.

The Subconscious functions as both the gateway to the Higher Self and as the messenger that conveys all our thoughts to the Higher Self. The Subconscious and the Higher Self are perfectly and seamlessly interwoven as a part of each other. When we become relaxed, a clear channel of communication opens between the Conscious, Subconscious, and the Higher Self. While each of these minds are present at all times, when we are in a deep state of relaxation, communication between these minds is at its clearest and most powerful level. It's also important to understand that this channel of communication works both ways. Not only do we communicate from the Conscious to the Subconscious and the Higher Self in order to create, but the reverse is true also. An example of communication coming from the Higher Self through the Subconscious and into the Conscious mind is Intuition. We all have intuitions and "gut feelings" that seem to magically pop into our minds. Intuitive and imaginative thoughts originate at the Higher Self level and move into our awareness at the conscious level of mind.

It is through accessing our Subconscious Mind that we are able to maximize our human potential and live our best lives. In each of the following chapters, I will discuss a different mode of accessing this illusive control station, and present simple techniques that you can use immediately to gain access to your Subconscious and modify your beliefs and habits. As with most Personal Development books, if you want to change something in your life, the you must TAKE ACTION. So I would encourage you to take at least ONE ACTION each day for the next 30 days, and you will see some great results!

CHAPTER 2

GOALS

To be successful in any area of life, you need a dream. Stop for a moment and think about what it is that you REALLY want. Then simply write your answer down, and viola! Don't look now, but you're actually setting goals! The starting point for any winner lies is simply DECIDING what they want. When you have a goal in mind, it's a bit like knowing the destination on a car trip, except that this is the trip of your LIFE. If you were to stop any car in the street, there is a good chance the driver can tell you their destination! If you were to stop any winner in the street, you will probably find they could tell you exactly where they were going. Winners have dreams and goals and essentially they are driving towards it as they live their lives every day. Very few people in the general population are consciously working towards their dream, with the same sense of direction and intensity as an Olympic athlete or a highly successful international businessman or woman.

THOSE WHO FOCUS ON BIG, JUICY GOALS ARE MORE LIKE TO BE HIGHLY SUCCESSFUL IN THEIR FIELD, BECAUSE THEIR FOCUS IN ON WHERE THEY WANT TO GO.

The good news is that I believe that we all have goals; it's just that most of the goals aren't very big, and we don't put enough energy into achieving our goals. Most people are working towards small goals, whether it is a small increase in wages, a holiday or a bigger car next year.

If you're not excited, your goal isn't big enough.

Having written goals is like having a shopping list in hand when you go into a supermarket. Without the list, you don't get half the things you want or need. Whereas when you go into a supermarket with a list, you tend to remain focused and ultimately get what you initially wanted. It's the same with writing goals for your business, sport or life. Your mind works more effectively when you write out a list of goals. It sees the goals on your list and then looks for the goals and opportunities to reach your goals throughout the course of each and every day. Of course not all goals are just found or spotted by your mind, so a list will help you focus on your priorities and actions.

Imagine someone heavily overweight who wanted to be a healthy weight. If they were to picture themselves slim or say "I want to be slim," their mind will bring up an image of them as slim and it actually keeps working until the goal picture becomes the real picture. Using the mind to conceive a goal helps you achieve a goal. However, this is the part that 95% of weight watchers get wrong. They don't set the goal correctly. They say, "I want to lose weight." It's a bit like saying "I don't want to miss this shot" instead of saying "I want to score the goal."

You can't start winning until you stop thinking about losing!
You've got to focus on what you DO want, not on what you don't want.

Humans have been designed for survival. Since cave man days we have been managing our progress by setting goals. When a caveman was hungry he set out with the goal of finding something to eat. His mind would help him achieve that goal in order to survive. Humans are really designed to set and achieve goals, but few humans fully utilize this precious ability. It is an interesting phenomenon, but it has been shown that when your mind sees a goal on your wall or in your mind, it then goes looking for it in your external world or "reality".

Your mind keeps working until the fantasy becomes reality.

Your brain has a highly specialized filtering system, called the Reticular Activating System (or RAS), which works like a metal detector at airport security. The goal of your RAS is to detect any important points and when it does, to raise the alarm and bring it to your attention. Your RAS is a filter that processes the thousands of pieces of 'incoming' information received every minute by your brain. Meanwhile the RAS ignores the mass amount of non-important information it receives but will identify and highlight any important information and subsequently bring it to your conscious attention. Your RAS needs to know your goals so it can identify anything relevant to those goals that is important to you.

The human body has an amazingly complex series of sensory collection systems—your eyes see everything, your ears hear everything, your skin feels everything, your nose smells everything and your tongue tastes everything—and then all this sensory information is filtered into your brain, every millisecond of every day! All day long, you are surrounded by an enormous quantity of both external and internal stimuli. But luckily, your RAS only informs you of the important stuff that you need to pay attention to. So when you first think about a goal, your mind will immediately add the goal to its "Important Information List", recognizing the information that it needs to focus on. From that moment on, anything related to achieving that goal or in some way connected with that goal is flagged by your RAS as important information.

Set a goal and your mind starts looking and recognizing key points.
Without a goal your mind is filtering and ignoring.

Your mind must KNOW your goals in order to be able to help you, and this is why you need to regularly look at your goals and remind the mind what it's looking for! If your mind isn't aware of your goals, you won't be aware of the opportunities that become available to you. If your RAS knows what your goals are, and it is regularly reminded of them, it will be continually scanning and searching for relevant information and opportunities, and it is more likely to make you aware of them, as opposed to filtering out all the positive opportunities along with all the extraneous details. You only consciously notice what your mind considers is important. If you have a list of goals that you review regularly (daily or several times a day), your mind will spot anything relevant to those goals and make you consciously aware of it. If you don't have goals, your mind will not make you aware when you pass a good opportunity. If your mind knows what your goal is and the RAS points out useful information and opportunities to you but you ignore them (for months or years), it will eventually 'drop' that goal from the "Important Information List". Even if you didn't mean to, you demonstrated to your mind through your actions, that the goal and opportunity wasn't important to you. If you give up on your goals, your mind will give up on your goals, and you will be blind to any future opportunities to achieve your goals.

Your mind is like a video camera on 'record' all day. It stores your life experiences every day in your mind, including all sensory information. The previous sensory information that is held in storage and the memories from past experiences, helps your mind identify new 'incoming' sensory information it receives during every day. Your mind is always recording, even when you're sleeping, which is why it is possible to record dreams. The powerful mind recorder stores all our thoughts and actions every day. So if you think about a goal or write it down just once, it is recorded. At this point, you may experience some resistance, and start thinking, "Is it REALLY necessary to write down all your goals to be successful? What's the POINT?" Research over the past 20 years has proven time and time again, that physically writing or typing your goals is much more effective than simply thinking about them. Writing helps you to clarify your goals to a greater degree than merely thinking about them—the physical act of writing a goal down effectively deepens your degree of commitment to each goal, when you make the extra effort to commit them to ink. Secondly, it can assist your focus by establishing your priorities and helping you to concentrate on doing things that are useful in moving you towards the achievement of your goals, in that you will be more aware of when you are wasting your time. And thirdly, written goals are simply more powerful than just 'thinking' goals because the act of writing the goal actually encourages you to clarify the vision of your goal more fully.

Thinking is something that most people don't do enough of. The process of active positive thinking is something that most people have heard of, but never actually do! Thinking is not an activity that requires a lot of physical effort or a lot of time. Thinking is something that most winners do and most losers don't do. We actually try to avoid thinking! From the moment we wake up, we turn the noise up. We are uncomfortable in silence. After we hit our teens, most of us avoid it completely. And as adults, we actively run from it! We seem to 'fill' any silent spaces in our lives with any kind and quality of noise.

Writing goals does work. In the course of your lifetime, some goals will come to you, seemingly delivered right onto your plate—but you still have to grab them! But these are more likely to be little goals. Rarely will a HUGE goal, one that exists out beyond your comfort zone, be so conveniently delivered to you—without some significant effort on your part. Your mind will give you opportunities to achieve your little goals AND your big goals. But you have to take the appropriate action. A big goal may require a big risk—are you prepared to take a risk for your goal? A big goal may need a big amount of hard work—are you willing to do it? What price are you willing to pay for your dreams?

"A dream doesn't become a reality through magic; it takes sweat, determination, and hard work."

~ Colin Powell, Former US Secretary of State ~

ONE SMALL STEP: RECOGNIZE YOUR PAST ACHIEVEMENTS

Once you set goals for the future it's easy to focus on them and forget what you have already achieved. You have achieved great things already! Some things you worked for and some just seemed to flow easily to you. Some things you have only thought about once, while other you may have thought about a lot. It's important to recognize your past successes, because that will help you create more believable goals to focus on today. Thinking about your past achievements puts you in the physical state of knowing that you CAN achieve your goals. Pause now, and identify the seven biggest goals you have ever achieved.

1. _____

2. _____

3. _____

4. _____

5. _____

6. _____

7. _____

Was it hard to remember these huge achievements? Do you make a note of your achievements every year, month or every week? Unless we write down our achievements, it's easy to miss our progress. It is situations like these that maintaining a personal journal becomes a valuable tool in tracking your progress, as it allows you to record how far you have come, providing you look back occasionally (notice I said OCCASIONALLY, and not CONTINUALLY)! There is a huge difference between looking back to learn from your past, and continually focusing on and re-living your past experiences. When was the last time you celebrated your achievements? Don't miss your greatness, CELEBRATE YOUR GREATNESS! But be honest—if you perform well below your ability, recognize that it's not really time to celebrate, and that it's time to set yourself a bigger, stronger goal and give yourself a good talking to! Then get on with it and choose a positive attitude to face the future.

Researchers in the USA looked at millionaires and billionaires, examining the differences between the two groups. One fascinating difference was that millionaires looked at their goals once a day and billionaires looked at their goals twice a day! They say 'it costs nothing to look', which is generally correct but the reverse is definitely true in this case. If you don't look, it will cost you! Having a date for your dreams is like giving a student a deadline for an assignment. All the action is last minute,and if you didn't set a deadline you'd never get it done!

Goals with deadlines are like dreams with delivery dates!

The mind is really good at recognizing things. One of the main reasons goal setting is so powerful is because your mind wants your internal picture (your GOAL) to be the same as your external picture (your CURRENT REALITY), kind of like the card-game 'Snap'. It will then set itself to attract a goal, recognize goal-related opportunities or work on a goal until you achieve a goal, without you consciously having to direct your attention every moment of the day.

An even more powerful way to introduce your dream to your mind is to actually physically visit it! If it's not possible to visit it in real life (eg: test drive the new car, walk through your dream house etc), then visit it through visualization. Get a picture of yourself standing beside your dream item (it may be a car/home/ job etc). I have put this activity to the test in my own life. When I was looking to build my first home, I visited a number of display homes, took photos of myself in my dream home and then posted those photos in my vision book. Several years later I recovered that particular vision book from a storage box, and was surprised to see that the home that I eventually built was almost an exact mirror of those photos I had posted in my book!

I've outlined why you need to set goals, why you need to write them down, why you need to look at them at least twice a day and why having pictures of your goals helps a lot!. Now I would like to emphasize the beauty and benefit of setting BIG goals. There are BIG benefits from having BIG goals! Most obviously, you might just achieve them! And even if you don't actually reach your goals, at least you won't waste your talents—instead, through the process of devising and writing goals, you are more likely to move out of your comfort zone and to achieve something greater than what you would had you not even attempted to dream a bigger dream.

The big benefits of working towards big goals: Amazing happiness, stretching your ability, increased passion, more energy, infectious enthusiasm, amazing achievement and actually creating the life you dream of! People who achieve great things tend to do so because they are powered by great dreams, while those who fail to achieve their fullest potential are more likely to NOT be 'big thinkers'. You have got to think big to achieve big.

Every business should have at least one big goal, and every person within the company must know what that goal is and what it means for them as individuals as well as the business as a whole. If everyone believes in the goal, then that makes it even more powerful. The method for choosing your big goal for a business is the same as the method for choosing the big goal for an individual person. American President John F. Kennedy set the big goal of being in space in 1961. It was a dream and it had a deadline. He said, "I regard that decision as among the most important decisions that will be made during my incumbency in the office of the Presidency." John F. Kennedy's famous "Moon Speech" the following year was brilliant, and it made Americans fully aware that they were all chasing the same dream.

"You always miss 100% of the shots you don't take!"
~ Wayne Gretsky—Ice Hockey Legend ~

You have no idea what you are capable of. Can you pause now and just consider what you THINK you might be capable of. Think BIG. REALLY BIG. Then double it and you're getting close. But in reality, you're not even warm. WE HAVE TO PUSH BEYOND OUR LIMITS BEFORE WE FIND OUR LIMITS. Living with unused ability can be likened to having giant wings but not realizing that we have them—let alone what they can be used for. It's only if we attempt to fly that we realize we have wings. And it's only when we start using our wings that we realize we CAN FLY.

The world is full of people who are all too eager to speak without thinking, and too scared to think deeply about their hopes and dreams. There are too many people working towards their retirement and not enough people working towards their dream. Ordinary people CAN achieve EXTRAORDINARY things. Most people think 'becoming a millionaire' is an "unrealistic goal", and yet hundreds of people become millionaires every year! Ordinary people CAN achieve extraordinary things. It all comes down to the point of power—the DECISION to make it so.

The people who achieve truly amazing things are the dreamers, often labelled 'unrealistic', like Sir Richard Branson, Lance Armstrong, Oprah Winfrey, Bill Gates, Steve Jobs and Henry Ford. How our world needs them! None of our heroes would have become heroes or achieved such great feats if they were "realistic people". So if you feel that your big goal is too scary for you to deal with, reassure yourself that you'll be able to get comfortable again soon enough. Winners set goals and then push themselves outside their comfort zone, even for only a short period of time.

Sir John Harvey-Jones is also of the view that we are capable of more than we think. In his timeless and classic book 'Making It Happen' he identified the importance of stretching beyond our comfort zones, both in work and in life generally. He stated, "The demands made on people always needs to be heavy. People at all levels of the organization can accomplish much more than they are asked to under normal conditions. Not only is it necessary organizationally to stretch others, but it is also necessary to stretch ourselves." How many times have you told yourself you could not do something but when you ultimately faced up and had a go, to your amazement you succeeded? I am firmly of the belief that most people in this world achieve only a fraction of what they are capable.

ONE SMALL STEP: WHAT IS YOUR BIG DREAM?

This is where you write down your dreams and goals.

Where do you want to drive your destiny to?

Grab your pen. Now it's time for you to stop reading and start doing!

Take at least 5-10 minutes to write down as many goals as you can. The best method is to write down as many goals as you can (pick a number between 20 and 40) and only stop when you have no other goals 'popping' into you head.

_____
_____
_____
_____
_____
_____
_____
_____
_____
_____
_____

_____
_____
_____
_____
_____
_____
_____
_____
_____
_____
_____
_____
_____
_____
_____
_____
_____
_____
_____
_____
_____
_____
_____
_____
_____
_____

Necessity is the mother of motivation.

Now read the following questions one at a time and think about your answer to each one. You may find these are new goals to add to your goals above or they may be the same. If you are still looking for the 'BIG one' the following questions may help you find your dreams and goals.

1. Describe your "Average Dream Day"—note I said Average Dream Day—this is not a highly exceptional, extra-ordinary day that comes along once in a lifetime—this is the kind of day you will experience every day, when your life is running perfectly.

_____

2. Describe your "Average Dream Year"

_____

3. If you could do ANYTHING, what would you do?

_____

_____

_____

_____

_____

_____

_____

_____

_____

_____

_____

_____

_____

_____

_____

4. If you had NO FEAR, what would you do?

_____

_____

_____

_____

_____

_____

_____

_____

_____

_____

5. If you KNEW you would NOT FAIL, what would you do?

_____

_____

_____
_____
_____
_____
_____
_____
_____
_____
_____
_____

6. If you won the Lottery, what would you do?

_____
_____
_____
_____
_____
_____
_____
_____
_____
_____
_____

7. If you had only ONE YEAR TO LIVE, what would you do with this year?

_____
_____
_____
_____
_____
_____
_____
_____

I love the question, "If you won the lottery, what would you do?" If you have ever had that uncomfortable experience that you know that you want to do something, but you have no idea what it should be, then you need to ask yourself this question. Ask yourself "What do I want to do?" every morning and every evening, and keep asking until you get an answer that you are inspired to take action on. For an even better results, try removing all limitations from yourself by asking "IF I COULD DO ANYTHING RIGHT NOW, WHAT WOULD I DO?" . . . And then go do it!

"A man is a success if he gets up in the morning, goes to bed at night, and in between he does what he wants to."
~ Bob Dylan ~

Well done—you are in the top 1% of people who write down their goals and think about what they really want . . . How cool it that? Now look at your list of goals and your answers to the questions above, and pick out your dream goal, your BIG GOAL. If you could have JUST ONE GOAL, what would it be? This is your BHAG—your Big Hairy Audacious Goal! Just thinking about this goal gets your heart racing and makes you excited, so you know it's something you REALLY want. Go for it! You really need to have a goal that motivates you. Having a big goal that not only excites you but also motivates you is ESSENTIAL to being a winner in life.

An English lady named Elaine was asked what she would do if she won the lottery. She promptly replied, "I would live in France." Once she identified her dream, she created a plan that would enable her to move her business and her family to the French countryside within 6 months. The key point here is that Elaine was able to implement her plan without having to wait for that illusive lotto win. Elaine's philosophy is this: "Decide what you want, and then work out how to do it NOW!" Decide what you can do without the money, but with some hard word or hard decisions. Don't wait, JUST DO IT! Life is so precious—don't waste any more of your heartbeats waiting for something to happen . . . DO IT NOW!

Look at your list of goals and dreams now, and pick your top 7 goals, including the "BHAG" (That's your Big Hairy Audacious Goal). Now write out these goals, in order of importance.

Importance	Goal	Due Date
1	I will take my family to Italy in July this year, and stay at _____ for 21 days.	Bookings by 1st May
2		
3		
4		
5		
6		
7		

Consider the dates that you wish to achieve your dreams by. It is so important to include a due by date when you're writing down your goals, because that is how you ground your dreams in reality. Go with your gut instinct. If you are too realistic, your big goal might not be quite so big and you could lose some of your motivation, so be careful on that front. When your dreams have dates, you know where you are going—you have a destination!

Write down your goals and get 7 corresponding pictures. Look at your goals and the related images twice a day—the more often you look at pictures of your goals, the more aware your subconscious will be of your goals, and the more your Reticular Activating System will subconsciously work to notice little opportunities in your everyday life that may help to turn your dreams into your reality.

IDENTIFY THE STEPS THAT WILL TAKE YOU TO YOUR DREAM

Once you have identified you Big Goals, you need to chunk it down into smaller, more manageable steps. Take the example of my family trip to Italy. That in itself could be seen as quite a big, scary and difficult goal.

But if I chunk it down a little, I could break it down into smaller steps by saying, to get to Italy, I will need to:

1. Decide what dates we need to fly.
2. Decide on an airline to fly with.
3. Get a quote of cost associated with the trip.
4. Decide on which villas we want to stay at, and what places we want to go to.
5. Organize time off from work.
6. Save up the money.
7. Book the flights.
8. Book the accommodation.
9. Decide on what type of clothes we need to take.
10. Learn the language.

And that's just a few things that came to mind straight up. Now I need to decide which of these steps I need to do first, and get into action. It is SO important never to leave the site of a decision, without having taken some kind of action. You can dream all day and all night—but if you never take any action, you will never get any action! You can't do everything at once, but you CAN do something right now. I suggest you focus your biggest effort on your BIG goal. Most winners have a dream and work on it. They have a priority. Focus on one thing at a time, your dream. The focus and direction of your front wheel will relate to the results you experience later in your back wheel. Where you steer is up to you.

ANOTHER SMALL STEP: TAKE CONTROL OF YOUR TIME

1. What makes you happy right now? Write a list of the things that you spend time on during a normal week that you really enjoy in the left hand column.
2. Now re-write them in order of importance in the next column.
3. Now put the minimum amount of time per day that you think you would need to spend to keep you happy and have time to spend working on your dream goals.
4. Now put down the maximum amount of time per week you would love to spend doing these things.

ACTIVITY	LEVEL OF IMPORTANCE	MAX TIME SPENT NOW	IDEAL MAX TIME
Family & Friends	1	1 hour	3 hours
Business	2	6 hours	3 hours
Networking	3	30 mins	1 hour
Play/Relaxation	2	1 hour	3 hours
Exercise	2	30 min	1.5 hrs
Sleep	2	7 hours	8 hours
Meditation	3	5 min	1 hour
Shopping	4	2 hours	1 hour

At this point, I would encourage you to understand that you don't have to spend every single moment of your day focused on your goals. Believe me, I've tried this, and it does not help you achieve your goals in the longer term—you are more likely to burn out and give up if you are OBSESSIVELY chasing your goals. Actually, you tend to REPELL your dream, because you're inadvertently focusing on the fact that you don't yet have it. The trick is to reward yourself when you have been focused, with some "fun time"—time where you do activities for the pure joy of doing them. This gives you the opportunity to recharge and reinvigorate yourself, filling your tanks so that when you do come back to your action plan, you are mentally, physically and emotionally invigorated—and it keeps your family and friends happy too!

When you strive for the jewels you want, don't drop the jewels you've got.

Now consider this: "Where else are you spending your time?" Where are you wasting time? Write a list of everything you spend time on, including sleep! Calculate your average week day and then calculate your average weekend. Look at the previous list, and highlight where you could reduce or cut time. Calculate the total amount of time you could spend/invest in working on your dream goal. Look at your goal list and your 'time waster' list and calculate the total amount of time you will 'invest' in your BIG goal. Now consider this question: "What is the most important use of my time?" Time is money, so you need to evaluate how you spend your time. Ask yourself "Is this a good investment of my time and money, or is it a waste of time and money?" Winners invest the majority of their time in their dream, because they don't want to risk NOT achieving it. To achieve your goal, you will have to make sacrifices. But to achieve your happiness you will have to carefully choose your sacrifices.

You could actually view your dream goals are as 'happy goals'. We are naturally drawn to create goals that would make us happy to achieve. The same goes for all your top seven goals. But what makes you "really happy" RIGHT NOW? You have to decide which goals would make you happiest, whether they are future 'dream goals' or current 'happy goals', which are in your life right now—and then prioritize your time accordingly. To achieve your dream goals, you'll need to maximize the use of your 'goal time' while still allowing for 'happy time'. Some people make the mistake of keeping so totally focused on their future goal (what they WANT) that they take their eye off the ball (what they've already GOT). Corporate culture is filled with sad stories of businessmen who were hugely successful in building business empires, but in the process, they lost either their families, their health or both!

Now it's time to look clearly at what NOT really going for your dreams has cost you so far—mentally, emotionally, spiritually, and financially. It's very important that you give full attention and commitment to this exercise, because it is vital for creating the kind of wealth that you deserve to have in your life.

ONE SMALL STEP: ESTABLISH YOUR PRIORITIES AND VOICE YOUR COMMITMENT

Answer the following questions in just two or three minutes. Don't take a lot of time thinking about your responses. Just write the first thoughts that come to mind. But play full out! You have to really go for it.

1. What is it cost of playing small and not really going for your dreams and not really playing full out in your life?

_____

_____

_____

_____

_____

_____

_____

_____

_____

2. What has that cost you so far in your life? What does it cost you spiritually? What does it cost you emotionally? And Financially?

_____

_____
_____
_____
_____
_____
_____
_____
_____
_____

3. What would it continue to cost you if you were to carry on playing small and not really going after your dreams? What would it cost you over the next year? Over the next three years? The next five years?

_____
_____
_____
_____
_____
_____
_____
_____
_____
_____

4. Then what would it cost you ULTIMATELY in your life? What would you miss out on? What's the ultimate price that you would have to pay for selling yourself short, playing small, and not going for your dreams?

_____
_____
_____
_____
_____

_____
_____
_____
_____
_____
_____
_____

5. What do you stand to GAIN by stepping up and making a commitment today to play FULL OUT, to follow your heart and to live your dreams? What's the ultimate benefit for you and your family?

_____
_____
_____
_____
_____
_____
_____
_____
_____

6. When you achieve that ultimate benefit, what will that allow you to Be, Do or Have?

_____
_____
_____
_____
_____
_____
_____
_____
_____

7. What's important to you about those benefits?

_____

_____

_____

_____

_____

_____

_____

_____

_____

8. How committed are you to that (How HOT is your Desire?)

_____

So now you're a little clearer about just how important your goals are to you, lets take a break and look within, and see how your internal conversations can guide you more accurately in the direction you want to go.

CHAPTER 3

INTUITION

Intuition, hunch, sixth sense, inner compass or gut feeling are all different names for the same thing. Your intuition is like an inner guide, which makes you pick one option over another. It shows up when you seem to "feel" confident choosing one path over another. The decision might be as simple as choosing between 'yes' or 'no' or the option could be open or unlimited.

Decisions are made all day every day. From the moment you wake up until the moment you decide to go to bed at night, you are making decisions. Every decision you make can influence your success or failure. Some decisions, which at first seem insignificant, can end up having a massive impact on your life. Then of course, there are the glaringly obvious big decisions, which are so significant you can guarantee success or failure. Your sixth sense can guide you when making these decisions.

Winners make decisions today that help them win tomorrow.

From the time of our birth, we develop the innate ability to instantly evaluate people as they who approach us or are situated in our immediate surrounds, on the basis of whether they are a friend (non threat) or a foe (threat). It is our mind's way of defending the body. Your mind is always on the lookout for threats, and your intuition is like your guardian angel. Upon meeting someone, you will get a 'sense' for the person. You might not trust them, take a dislike to them, or alternatively, you may click with them and feel instantly at ease in their company. The offending person might not even say anything 'wrong,' but you somehow 'sense' whether to like/dislike or trust/distrust them. A similar phenomenon of being able to sense potentially harmful people also translates to identifying safe and potentially harmful decisions. You get a 'sense' for what the best decision is in a given situation. You might have information which is complementary to your decision, or it may be the opposite. Nevertheless, you experience a 'feel' for the right decision.

People that listen to their intuition are believed to be luckier in life, according to Professor Richard Wiseman. He set out to scientifically discover the differences between people who are lucky and those who are unlucky. It took him eight years to complete his research into the subject and his book "The Luck Factor", but it makes for great reading.

Professor Wiseman identified four principle ways of thinking which 'make' people lucky:

1. They Appear to Maximize Chance Opportunities—Lucky people are skilled at creating, noticing, and acting upon chance opportunities. They do this in various ways, including networking, adopting a relaxed attitude to life and by being open to new experiences.

2. Lucky People Are More In Tune with Their Hunches—Lucky people make effective decisions by listening to their intuition and gut feelings. In addition, they take steps to actively boost their intuitive abilities, for example, meditating and clearing their mind of other thoughts.

3. Lucky People Expect Good Fortune—Lucky people are certain that the future is going to be full of good fortune. These expectations become self-fulfilling prophecies by helping lucky people persist in the face of failure, and shaping their interactions with others in a positive way.

4. Lucky People Are Able To Turn Bad Luck into Good—Lucky people employ various psychological techniques to cope with and often even thrive upon, the ill fortune that comes their way. For example, they spontaneously imagine how things could have been worse, do not dwell on ill fortune, and take control of the situation.

If your right brain is telling you something,
don't wait ten years for the left-brain to tell you the same thing!

As mentioned in the previous chapter, the mind stores all the sensory information it has received, and this information is subsequently accessed by your mind to help you make intuitive decisions. In an experiment, people were shown 1000 photographs, one after the other at a speed of about one per second. The psychologists then added 100 new photographs with the original 100 and mixed them all up. Everyone was asked to identify those they had not seen before and everyone (regardless of intelligence or memory level) was able to identify almost every 'new' photograph and 'old' photograph. The brain stores all visual and written information, but we find it easier to recall images. Which explains why it can be easier to remember someone's face than their name!

Knowing WHERE to focus your time every week is important, and having that 'knowledge' can be the difference between a profitable business and an unprofitable business or a winning athlete and a losing athlete. An individual may be able to access that knowledge intuitively or learn that knowledge again from scratch—essentially that means they can either take the easy way or the hard way. As children we all grow up talking to ourselves, mainly out loud. However, because we get laughed at when we continue this practice as we get older, we tend to talk to ourselves silently instead. We continue to talk to ourselves everyday, almost every minute of every day, but mostly only in our minds. It's not always obvious to us, but this is our intuition talking with us, and we're not always aware of our intuition until it is pointed out.

Now that you're aware that you're carrying on continuous conversations (with yourself), it's important to maintain a positive approach to those conversations. If you are able to stay physically and mentally relaxed prior to making a big decision, reassure yourself that you WILL make a great intuitive decision, and don't be afraid to make mistakes—they are great if you view them as learning opportunities. Often, you learn more from mistakes than you do from your outright successes. Reassure yourself that there is a small chance you will make a mistake, but always remember that your mistakes are great lessons. Most people pat themselves on the back when they win. But the path to winning involves lots of losing. Winners win a lot, but often this occurs only after they lose a lot. Why don't you try appreciating your mistakes, and make sure that you learn from them the first time you make them!

Learn from your mistakes, and then don't make them again

There are many ways to improve your intuitive success, the most effective being to increase the amount of Down Time or Stillness Time in your day. By participating in calming exercises, such as Meditation, Yoga or Tai Chi, you not only receive physical benefits of the actual exercise, but you increase your awareness of your own Inner Voice. Even short periods of solitude and contemplation will provide you with the space to access your intuitive wisdom. By improving your self awareness, you will come to recognize the instances when it's your Higher Self talking, and when it's your Ego trying to keep you "safe". This is the time when you really need to learn how to differentiate between the different voices in your head. One quick way to clarify this is to allocate specific voice types and tones to different voices. For example, when you recognise that your Ego is talking, I give my Ego a whiney, nasal kind of voice. Whereas my Higher Self has a soft, loving and calm voice that instantly builds trust.

One way to strengthen the sound of your internal voice is to give it attention, and you can do this most effectively by journalling your thoughts and experiences on a regaular basis (daily or twice daily is recommeded). This regular habit gives you the opportunity to access your deepest thoughts and feelings, and to get them out onto paper, effectively purging them from your body and thus releasing their hold on you emotionally.

CHAPTER 4

VISUALIZATION

Visualization is one of the most powerful techniques known to man. Visualization is like a 'mental movie' of a future event that you direct in your mind. Positive visualization is used by every winner in sport and business. Successful people create an image or 'movie' in their mind of the results they want BEFORE they even start their physical activity. Sometimes they may have visualized their goals for years. Visualization is a common skill we all use on a regular basis; to achieve anything, to do anything, we first need to 'see' ourselves doing it. So visualization is not something strange or difficult or esoteric, but it is something we all constantly use in order to function in the world . . . . we all can visualize. The trouble is, many people use visualization NEGATIVELY in that they imagine all the bad things that could happen, and then HOPE they don't!

The important thing to realize is that we human beings are a lot like guided missiles—we move in the direction of our regular and consistent thoughts and imaginings; we move toward what we picture in our mind—particularly what we picture with vividness and strong feeling. Whenever we associate a vivid picture with a strong feeling, it has a magnetic attraction—so be careful of what you picture with feeling, because you will eventually be pulled in that direction.

A classic example of this process in action is given by the tennis player who serves a fault with his first serve. As he prepares to hit his second serve, an image comes to mind of double faulting—perhaps even recalling a previous time when he had done so. As he pictures this memory, he sees it vividly, and of course feels the embarrassment he experienced initially. He then proceeds to tell himself, "Now I don't want to double fault!".

But of course it's too late . . . . he has already visually programmed himself with clear pictures and powerful feelings to do just that! As the ball is tossed, he tenses up because he's afraid of failing, and then watches with dismay as it flies straight into the net. Why did this happen? Despite all his self talk NOT to hit a double fault, he does just that. Has anything like that ever happened to you? Have you ever commanded yourself not to do something, only to find it happening despite all your conscious efforts? Maybe you've said to yourself, "Now this time I'm not going to get nervous and stammer when I speak today", and yet you did! This is an excellent example of the power of visualization, as seen from a negative perspective.

The Mental Movie is an extremely powerful technique that has been used by famous "greats" like Walt Disney, Mohammed Ali, Nelson Mandela, Jack Nicklaus and Steven Spielberg. And if you use this technique too, it will probably be very successful for you! Creating a 'mental movie' can be done with your eyes open or closed. It can be used to win a competition, sink a putt, walk down a catwalk, finalize a sale or make a great presentation. There are unlimited ways in which it can be used. I will highlight some of the most powerful and relevant details here, but the rest I'll leave to your imagination. Use your imagination to create a 'Mental Movie' of what you want to happen and what you want to achieve. Remember, YOU are the director of this movie, so make it a very positive, successful picture and make sure you give yourself the gift of a very happy ending!

When you are short of time, the most important aspect of a 'mental movie' is to create and visualize the end result that you most desire. If you want to succeed, picture the 'happy ending' before you even begin! Successful people often can be heard to say something like "I pictured myself winning" or "I had a vision of it before I completed it." Before you start, picture the end! Make a mental movie of everything from the specific goals you want to achieve, to meetings you wish to run smoothly, to vacations you dream of taking. If you are unable to picture your whole day, just picture the happy ending and feel yourself falling into bed, utterly satisfied with the results of your day.

The first time you attempt do something new, you may be nervous and your subsequent performance may be below average. The second time, you may still be slightly nervous and perform on average, the third time, you may feel excited and your performance may be good, but the fourth time, you may feel more relaxed and your subsequent performance may even be great. By practicing, you are improving. But 'doing' does not lead to gold medal performances or everyone would be a winner. Practice does not make perfect—only PERFECT PRACTICE makes for perfect results. If you do a positive visualization several times, you will calm your nerves and increase your level of excitement. Visualizing your performance of the 'first time' completing any task will improve your performance by reducing your nerves and giving you the confidence that you CAN complete the task. You may have used this technique already in some areas of your life, but did you know that these principles can be easily applied to ANY area of your life?

There's a wonderful book by Tim Gallwey called 'The Inner Game of Tennis', where he talks about the concept of the two selves. Tim was a tennis coach, and he noticed people talking to themselves on the court, and from this he suggested that we actually have two 'selves' or two different parts of the mind. The First Self is the Conscious part of the mind or 'Commander', the part of us that is always telling us to "Keep your wrist firm", "Watch the ball", "Follow through", or whatever. The Second Self is our Non-Conscious 'Worker' self, is the part of us that receives and acts on those commands. Now the interesting thing about the Second Self—the 'Worker' part of our mind, is that it understands vivid pictures and images better than it does words. It's similar to a computer in that it understands a particular programming language . . . however the programming language of The Second Self is not MS DOS or WINDOWS XP, but rather vivid visual images. Self Two is a very competent servant and it accurately follows the instructions given to it that are embedded in the language the person uses to communicate within themselves and with others.

However most people try to program Self Two with words—they verbally command their body to do something without having a clearly visualized and precise picture of exactly what they want to happen. But it just doesn't work effectively—it's a bit like talking in a foreign language. If I spoke with you in a language you had never heard before, I couldn't expect you to fully understand the entire sentence. It's just the same when you try to 'talk' to your body—it just doesn't understand the words you use.

The way to command, or 'program' your body effectively is to use VIVID MENTAL IMAGES, particularly images associated with strong feeling.

This concept is supported by comments from many champion sportspeople. Legendary golfer Jack Nicklaus has been quoted as saying "I never hit a shot, even in practice, without having a clear, in-focus picture of it in my mind." US Diver Greg Louganus, after hitting his head on the diving board in one of his dives in the 1988 Olympics, was asked by one of the television crews if he wanted a copy of the dive to see where he went wrong. He refused, saying he didn't even want to consider the possibility that Greg Louganus could hit his head on a diving board! Now that's maintaining a positive focus!

You want to have a positive focus, and you want to communicate with your body in a way that it understands—by giving it clear, vivid images. It could be said that your level of performance is directly related to the precision of your visual communication, and the level of trust you can establish between your Self One and Self Two.

There is overwhelming scientific and anecdotal evidence which demonstrates the undeniable fact that visualization can improve your sports performances as there are numerous scientific studies which have shown its effectiveness. Feedback from athletes has shown that they improved their performance from 10% to 50%! One classic example of the extraordinary power of visualization has been provided by the experiences of Colonel George Hall when he was captured by the Vietnamese in the war and incarcerated in a prisoner of war camp for seven years—five and a half of which were spent in solitary confinement. Prior to the war, Colonel Hall was an avid golfer, playing off a handicap of four, and to keep himself from going crazy in prison, every day he would visualize playing a round of golf. He would play each shot, and each hole in his mind, and every day he'd play a different golf course.

When Colonel Hall was finally released and returned to the USA, he was invited to play in a celebrity Pro-Am tournament, and despite being underweight and suffering from malnutrition from his ordeal, he hit a round of 76 . . . right on his handicap, despite not having held a golf club for over seven years! That is the power of the visualization process, and it works because it has a measurable, physiological effect on our body. When you visualize doing a movement, play, stroke, shot, or performance, there is a measurable response by the specific muscles used in that activity in response to your imagined movements. For instance, in order to do a tennis serve in reality, a specific 'program' of neuromuscular circuits has to fire in order for that to happen. However, if I just vividly imagine doing a tennis serve, it's been found that micro-muscular stimulation occurs in those same muscles used to do the serve in 'reality'.

In fact, neurologically, your body can't tell the difference between a 'real' experience, and a vividly imagined one. You consciously know one experience is real and the other is imagined, but at the cellular level, your body can't tell the difference. For example, think of the last time you had a nightmare . . . . and now think of a time you had a fright in 'reality'. Was the fear you experienced in the dream any different from the fear you experienced in response to the 'real' event? It wasn't was it? Your heart still pounded the same and your hands still felt clammy. Perhaps you even jerked your arm up in the dream in response to the imagined events! It was only a dream, but your body still responded like it was real didn't it? Because there is this muscular response to visualized activity, it makes it possible to 'program in' desired shots, strokes, plays, movements, behaviors, and even emotional responses prior to doing them. In other words you can 'groove' a desired response into your body at a cellular level, creating a 'muscle memory' of what you want your body to do. To take this point a little further, visualization allows you to practice your techniques perfectly—without error, thus allowing you to memorize the optimum neural pathway for future successful performance.

The art of visualization is a transformation technique you can use to obtain anything you want in life: love, prosperity, self-confidence, weight loss, a new job or car—whatever you wish. Imagining is a very precise methodology that can transform your life, but there are certain rules governing it.

Here, then, are the steps to follow to create your own reality through creative visualization.

1. Get Quiet and Relax: Find a quiet place where you will be totally undisturbed and can completely relax. The more deeply you can relax, the more effective your visualization will be. Never try to visualize when you are surrounded by potential interruptions—you are simply wasting your time and energy, because even if you are not actually interrupted, you will not be fully relaxed because part of you will be WAITING to be interrupted. If you can find no other place where you can be undisturbed for 10 minutes, lock yourself in the bathroom!

2. Use only Positive Phrases: Make up a short, concise summary of exactly what you want, and always state it in the positive tense.

For example, if you are working on weight loss, never say "I will not be fat". This vibrates the cells in your brain connected with image of obesity and reinforces the idea that you are overweight. Even though this may be true, don't strengthen the image by reminding yourself of it. You would be better off saying, "I am becoming slimmer every day." If you feel inadequate, don't say, "I am overcoming my inferiority complex," because that leads you to focus on your inferiority complex, effectively increasing the level of anxiety you feel. Instead, say "I am becoming more confident every day."

Imagine that an obese lady posts a picture of a hippopotamus on her fridge door, where she glances at the picture many times each day. In effect, this seemingly harmless action is actually communicating powerfully to her subconscious mind that she thinks she looks like a fat hippo. However, a picture of a slender model from a fashion catalogue with her own face photo-shopped onto the model's body can quite effectively let her subconscious know what she DOES want (to be a healthy slender weight), instead of reinforcing what she DOESN'T want (to gain weight).

In dealing with specific things you desire, you can name a time limit; "By this spring, I will have my new car." "I am now losing 1 kilogram per week, and by Christmas I will weigh 75 kilograms." or "I will start my new job by the first of March."

Your positive statements can be written on 3x5 cards and placed by your bedside, on the bathroom mirror, on the dashboard of your car on in your wallet—any place where you can see them frequently and repeat them, thus giving your subconscious mind ample reminders throughout the day. If you can visualise your desire at bedtime and fall asleep holding that thought, your subconscious will be able to work on it all night long, without any interference, and the process will be more effective.

3. <u>Make Your Movie Logical:</u> The key to getting a message into the subconscious mind is: If it's logical, it lodges; and if it lodges, you're hooked! Remember, logical doesn't necessarily mean TRUE.

If, when you were 6 years old, you were told by your parents that you were awkward, clumsy and not as bright as your brother or sister, that suggestion would probably have made sense to you. After all, a parent is a very powerful authority figure in a child's life, so surely they knew what kind of person you were. Our personalities are formed by what we are told about ourselves in the process of growing up, even if it wasn't true. If something is said to you that appears to be logical and you have no way to refute it, it becomes accepted by your subconscious and becomes part of you.

On the other hand, if a statement does not appear logical to you, the conscious mind will simply not accept it, or will refute it, and it will not get past the psychic barrier into the subconscious. Thus, if your conscious mind cannot fully believe and trust the authenticity of your image, it will not be accepted by your subconscious. For instance, if you wish to make some money, you should not say: "I am going to earn one million dollars by the end of the year." For most of us, this is completely illogical, so the subconscious will not accept it. If you want to lose weight, you shouldn't say: "I'll lose 10 kilograms by the end of this month," because you probably won't be able to convince yourself you can.

4. Be Specific In Your Request: The more detail you can bring into your image, the easier it will be for your subconscious to carry it out.

The subconscious mind is quite literal, and it needs to be given accurate directions. Of course, this is not always possible, but whenever it is, take the time to clarify specific details of your image. If you are looking for a new job, you may not be able to specify the particular building you would like to work in, but you can imagine yourself smiling and happy as you walk around in your new office.

For example, if you would like to have a new house, identify in advance all the things that you want to have in your home. Would you like a garden or a small yard that needs little care? Do you want a 2 car garage, lots of storage space, a large kitchen, three bedrooms, two baths, a fireplace, and a swimming pool? Be specific, but here again, make it logical. Don't ask for a house that is obviously beyond your means, because that is simply creating an unnecessary resistance to your obtaining that house, thus making it illogical for you to obtain it.

This process, known as Pre-Paving can be applied to any situation. A lady called Jenny lived in Sydney, and she planned to move interstate to Melbourne to work with a different division in her company. Jenny knew little about the new city, having only driven through it a couple of times. She didn't have any friends there and had no one to advise her on a good location in which to live. But instead of just driving around aimlessly in her car looking for an apartment, Jenny sat down one morning and typed the following:

I am going to Melbourne tomorrow to find an apartment that:

- Is quiet, so that I can relax undisturbed when I'm not working.
- Is close to my place of work.
- Is in a good neighbourhood where I feel safe.
- Is spacious and clean.
- Is bright and cheery and has lots of windows.
- Allows pets.
- Is in a price range of $_____ to $_____"

Jenny closed her eyes for a few minutes and imagined herself walking around in her new apartment feeling happy and content. Then Jenny turned the image over to the Universe, knowing that it knew the area much better than she did and could lead her to the place she desired. The following day, Jenny flew to Melbourne, and by that evening, she had put down a deposit on an apartment that met her specifications exactly, except that the price was somewhat higher than she had wished—and this was only because her range hadn't been logical or realistic!

In the past when Jenny had moved, she searched for weeks for places to live by trying to do it solely on her own without asking for help from the great powerhouse of knowledge within. But she had now learned that the method of directing and ordering her life by working with Spirit in a harmonious partnership is so much easier than doing things with her limited conscious mind. If you can learn to do EVERYTHING in cooperation with the Universe, your life can be so much simpler.

5. Take Enough Time: How long will it take to manifest your image? This is a variable that depends on your ability to concentrate and visualise and also on the severity of the challenge. Naturally, if you are trying to change lifelong feelings of inferiority, it will take some time; you can understand that five minutes of visualisation won't erase 30 years of negative thinking.

It has been established that it takes at least 33 seconds, as a bare minimum, for a suggestion to reach the subconscious mind. That's why TV commercials are usually at least that long. Also, psychologists have determined that, on the average, it takes about 21 days to change a habit. The same principle applies to images. But as your ability to visualise becomes perfected through repetition, you will find that many of your images will manifest sooner. Some people have reached a point where, through continued practice, some of their images come true within a few days, or even hours. How often should you visualise? A good goal to set is to practice 2 to 3 times per day for 10 to 15 minutes per session. The more you practice and develop your power of visualisation, the faster your images will come true.

Feeling and emotion profoundly affect the amount of time it takes to get an idea into the subconscious mind. When something is said to you that has an intense emotional impact, it slams into the subconscious the instant you hear it. If, for example, a parent or teacher or boss says, "You're really stupid," that thought immediately penetrates your subconscious mind. Unfortunately, when you begin working on changing a powerful suggestion like that, the same emotion is not behind it that was there when you originally heard it, so it takes longer to change, and requires multiple repetitions of the opposite concept (for every negative comment you hear, it has been proven that you need to hear 17 positive comments to compensate for that negative one!)

6. Experience the Feeling: An important aspect of an image is the EMOTION behind it. The more feeling you can get into your visualisation, the more convinced your subconscious will be that this is actually happening to you. ACT AS IF you actually HAVE the thing you desire and let your body experience the feelings you would have if you did.

For example, if you wish to lose weight, get the feeling of how happy you will be wearing clothes that were formerly too tight for you, hearing people congratulate you on your weight loss, looking at yourself in the mirror and feeling very proud of yourself. If you want a new car, imagine how good you will feel driving it down the freeway or pulling up in front of a friend's house in it. Remember, the subconscious can't tell the difference between something that is vividly imagined and something that is happening in reality, so very soon it will make it a reality for you, provided, of course, that it's logical. The more capable you are of living in the feeling of the dream fulfilled, the greater your capacity to actually receive your desire.

7. <u>Take Some Action on the Physical Plane</u>: You must impress on your subconscious that you mean business.

If, for example, you are working on weight loss, cut down on your food intake. If you're eating like a horse, you can visualise all day, and nothing will happen, because your subconscious is getting a double message. If you wish to get a new job, begin looking at the classified ads, sending out resumes, and networking with well-placed friends. If you want to be in a relationship, go out to places where there is an opportunity to meet the type of person you wish to spend time with.

One day I visited a friend Ellie, and found her living room full of boxes containing most of her belongings. Ellie was working her way through college and could only afford to live in a noisy apartment building filled with other students whose stereos blared day and night. She claimed that she could no longer put up with the noise and she was planning to move to a quieter building and get a room by herself. When asked how that was going to be possible on her limited income, she replied "Well, I have learned that if you want something to happen in your life, you first have to create a clear mental image, so I've been visualising a new apartment every day. And I decided that packing up everything I don't immediately need would be taking action to convince my subconscious mind that I'm serious, so that it will help me find a better place to live. Even if I have to stay here a few more months, I'm acting as if I'm moving, and that makes me feel better!" Ellie's subconscious did indeed receive her message and her mental movie became a reality shortly after. Within a few weeks, Ellie found an apartment for herself, close to the college, at only slightly more rent than she had already been paying.

8. In order for an image to manifest, you must CONCENTRATE intensely on it. This acts as a protective mechanism, effectively preventing all the little fleeting thoughts we have from automatically manifesting in our lives. If all the 'unimportant' thoughts did manifest immediately, we'd all be sorry for many of the things we created through careless thinking. When something doesn't happen on schedule, our tendency is to indulge in negative thinking.

For instance, if our partner doesn't arrive home at the usual time, often our first reaction is to begin worrying that he or she has been in an accident. Most of the time, we tend to think the worst, not the best. This sends out negative energy to the individual, and although it doesn't actually create the situation, it certainly doesn't help things. The best action under such circumstances is to sit down and take a few moments to visualise the person completely surrounded by a beautiful white light protecting them from any adverse forces. This is an ancient metaphysical method of psychic protection used for centuries to insulate a person from negative thoughts and forces. Then, visualise your loved one smiling, perfectly safe, coming in the front door. Strong concentration is necessary to manifest an image and the greater your ability to concentrate, the sooner your image will manifest for you. Concentration is an ability that can be developed; it is a learned skill just like any other. Training your mind day after day to focus on a particular image is a good way to develop your ability to concentrate.

ONE SMALL STEP: Visualize Your Life As A Perfectly Written Script

Sit in a quiet place, totally relaxed, and close your eyes. Step outside yourself. See yourself as an independent observer, watching from a distance. Now see yourself sitting in a movie theatre, watching what is taking place on the screen. See clearly the motives and agendas of the other people involved in the scene. You are the scriptwriter and the director—what would you have the hero of the movie do? It is totally in your hands. You can make a dispassionate decision. How do you want the characters to behave? Now write the script and give the direction. Make it an enjoyable and productive experience. See yourself with all the qualities you desire and deserve. One of the constant problems that arise is that others want you to be in their film. They want to direct your reality through the lens of their reality. Resist that temptation and retain control for yourself—Stay In Your Own Power.

Do not get caught up in the mistaken belief that you are not good enough now, but that in the future things will somehow be better. This way of thinking will instantly drain you of all your positive and constructive energy in this moment. You already HAVE the green pastures now because there is nothing but the present. It is now that you are in the green pastures, and by lying down and slowing down, you can experience these pastures more closely. You ARE surrounded by abundance. Whatever you experience in life, it will always be in the present for you. You have to live fully in the present. Live every second as an eternity. You must act in the moment with all of the integrity, honesty and commitment that you can muster. Do that now, not some time off in an imagined future and you will most certainly create the life of your dreams.

Don't bring the hurts and guilt of the past into your present experience. The past is just as much a part of your imagination as the future. You think the past has some basis in fact, but it is all in your imagination. If it doesn't exist in your imagination, then where does it exist? If the past and future exist in your imagination, what makes you think that the PRESENT doesn't also? Where does the present lie? It lies in performing an action with awareness.

During the day, place your mind in an environment surrounded by abundance. Be aware of the illusion of time. The vision that you hold clearly in your mind should be THAT YOU ARE SURROUNDED BY ALL THAT YOU NEED. Give thanks for all that you have. Don't bemoan what you perceive as a deficiency of any kind. Focus on what you have, and not on what you don't have. Even a millionaire can perceive deficiency if he or she perceives there is something which is beyond their reach.

In summary, here are the steps for creating your own reality through imagery:

1. Phrase it positively
2. Make it logical
3. Be specific
4. Take enough time and do it well
5. Visualise the end result
6. Step into the feeling that you already have your desire
7. Take some action on the physical plane
8. Never manipulate the will of another
9. Repetition and concentration will speed up the manifestation of your desire.

Imagination is the key to all creativity and to all changes in your life! It's not faith that makes all things possible, it's imagination. If you can imagine it, you can have it. By sustaining mental images of any kind (good or bad), you will eventually bring about their manifestation in the physical world. You ARE what you imagine yourself to be! Whether you think you can, or you think you can't, you're always right.

> *"Argue for your limitations, and you get to keep them."*
> ~ Richard Bach, Illusions ~

All of the world's great men and women have used the power of imagination to create their successful lives. They have become great because they dared to imagine grand achievements. They constantly pictured in their minds what they wanted and eventually brought them into being. Whatever is occurring now in your life is the result of an image in your mind, and whatever will happen in the future will be the result of YOUR images, not someone else's. This requires you to make a correct image of what you want to see happen in your life or personality, and turn that image over to the Universe to manifest.

We are all responsible to some degree for all that happens to us, even though it's often easier to blame someone or something else. Of course there are some circumstances beyond our control. But, if we have knowledge of how the mind works, we will recognise that the way we think and feel has an intimate connection with what is happening to us.

If we get up in the morning thinking it's going to be a bad day with nothing going right, then that is probably what will occur. Our thoughts go out into the Universe in the form of vibrations and attract to us exactly what we are sending out. If you are always surrounded by difficulties, the solution is to change the picture in your mind and imagine a more positive, fulfilling life.

Creative visualisation is the technique of using your imagination in a systematic, structured way to create what you want. Of course, we all use our imagination constantly, usually in an unconscious, haphazard or negative fashion. Worry, for example, is an extremely powerful image, and worried thoughts are always negative and destructive. Every time you fret about not getting the raise you want, possibly getting laid off, having a car accident, or not making your sales quota, you are programming your mind destructively. Since we have been taught so many negative concepts about ourselves, we automatically expect and IMAGINE that we will have difficulties, limitations, and misfortunes, thus bringing it into being.

Properly directed, imagination is the key to the doorway of success, love, health, abundance, satisfying relationships, self-confidence, and greater self-expression. All we need to do is become consciously aware of what we are creating, and change the programming if we don't like it.

Everyone has a basic concept about themselves, formed mainly by the ideas others gave us in early life, and also by the feedback we receive from people in our everyday lives. Unfortunately, many people's basic concept of themselves includes ideas such as failure, rejection, inferiority, ill health, worthlessness, financial instability, and other destructive thoughts.

We place our own limitations upon ourselves, and it's nothing more than an idea operating in the subconscious mind. Granted, many of these negative ideas were given to us by others when we were too young and too helpless to reject them. But now that we are adults, we can change them and reprogram our minds by the same process.

Your future is determined by the thoughts you think today.
What you think you are—YOU ARE!!!
Therefore, you can BECOME whatever you would like to be.

Many people are fond of stating that they are being "realistic," but they don't realise that, in so doing, they lock themselves into the statistical world, invariably bowing before the dictates of statistics and "facts" and believe that what happens to them is just the result of random chance.

We are constantly being programmed to statistics, such as "X number of people will die of cancer this year" or "Jobs these days are hard to get because many companies are still laying people off". Of course these may be facts. The statistical world is a reality because there are people who will make those statistics come true. They are people who have little control over their lives because they know nothing about the power of their own minds, and they are the helpless victims of life's vicissitudes. One who is able to think positively, however, and control his or her own thoughts, need not be caught in the trap of statistics. Such a person can consciously be superior to the "Slings and arrows of outrageous fortune."

In making images for the things you desire, you must be careful not to discuss them with people who cannot share your vision. A negative person can totally destroy your image by causing you to doubt its credibility. Holding an image of your desire takes a great deal of energy, especially when the odds may be against you achieving it. You have to work hard enough at overcoming your own doubt without allowing others, who do not understand the power of the mind, to influence you. When you remove all doubt that you WILL receive what you have imagined, it is sure to come to you. Believe in your images with all your strength, and don't allow nonbelievers to distort or destroy your faith by quoting statistics, or telling you all the reasons you cannot achieve them.

Creating what you want in life depends upon the use of the most potent force in the world: IMAGINATION. By sustaining mental images of any kind—good or bad—you will eventually bring about a physical effect. Unfortunately, our educational system stifles imagination by placing all the emphasis on rational thought. This may be one of the reasons our young people are so bored with school. If you have a child with an active imagination, you have a potential genius, because all creative people have highly developed imaginations. That is the source of their ideas, the realm of the inner life. Einstein once stated: "Imagination is more important than knowledge," adding that many of his ideas came to him while he was daydreaming or fantasising, and not while he was applying his intellect to a problem.

Many coaches today use the transformational technique of visualisation as a significant part of their athletes' training regimen. Charles Garfield, a former weightlifter and psychologist at the University of California, reported in Brain/Mind Bulletin (March 1980), that he had used visualisation with Olympic hopefuls to optimise their athletic performance. "The key," Garfield stated, "is to visualise with the clarity necessary to really FEEL yourself in the situation. The Central Nervous System doesn't know the difference between deep, powerful visualisation and the event itself, so the physical followup of the actual event is merely an after-the-fact duplication of an event already performed and completed in imagery."

Visualisation worked superbly for Chris Evert, now retired, who was a top-seeded professional tennis player. Before every match she sat down, relaxed, and visualised her every move, seeing herself return every one of her opponent's volleys and eventually winning the match. Her impressive record validates the effectiveness of this approach.

Imagery works because the subconscious cannot tell the difference between something that is strongly imagined and something that is actually taking place in the physical world. Anatomists have proven that there are pathways between the part of the brain where we store our pictures, and the autonomic nervous system that controls involuntary activities such as breathing, heart rate, and blood pressure. There are also pathways from the autonomic nervous system to the glands, such as the pituitary and adrenals. This means that a picture in our minds has an impact on every cell in our bodies. Thinking is not only an action of the mind, but an action of the entire body.

In his book 'The Body of Life', Thomas Hanna writes:

> "The nature of our thinking activity automatically determines the nature of our bodily activity . . . When we think the same thoughts of revenge over and over again, we are activating the muscles and glands of our bodies over and over again. When we repeat the same thoughts of disappointment over and over we are repeatedly stamping their motor power into the tissues of our body until they sag in forlornness."

By understanding this intimate connection between mind and body, we can use this knowledge to rejuvenate ourselves both physically and mentally, through the use of positive images. The Sub-conscious is all knowing and all-healing, and it will take excellent care of you, if you give it a fair chance! It never sleeps, if it did, you would not wake up in the morning because your subconscious takes care of your breathing, the circulation of your blood, your digestion, and every other bodily function while your conscious sleeps.

All you have to do is repeatedly tell your subconscious what you want, and it will then set about producing it. Unfortunately, instead of working positively to achieve what they want, many people start worrying about NOT getting it. This sends out negative energy, and you end up holding a picture in your mind that you won't obtain the desired result. You can add more negative energy to that by telling your friends you wish you could have this or that, but probably won't be able to. Then they, in turn, also hold the negative image. In this way, you keep constantly giving a message to your subconscious mind, NOT to bring you what you desire. The subconscious is a fertile field; whatever you plant is what you will reap.

Most people believe that wealth is the result of years of hard work and careful saving, unless one has inherited a fortune. This is a delusion. Statistics indicate that the majority of people in Western society, after spending the major part of their lives in work they sometimes didn't even enjoy, end up barely able to survive on social security and a small pension, if they have one at all. Reprogramming your ideas about money will attract it to you far more quickly than working a 12 hour day and diligently saving every dollar. The road to riches is paved with strong, positive ideas, held constantly in the mind, eventually attracting an abundance of money into your life. Accumulating wealth is the result of an attitude, and not the outcome of hard labour; changing your attitude is the key to becoming rich.

Your inner feeling about money determines whether or not you will have it, because that to which you give your attention is what manifests in your life. If you focus attention on the LACK OF MONEY and the FEAR OF POVERTY, then that is the experience that you are reinforcing and that subsequently becomes your reality. All human life is created by the human mind, and those who believe they deserve to be wealthy CAN create it.

A common myth about money is that there isn't enough for everybody. This is ridiculous because there are billions of dollars in the US Treasury alone, and YOU deserve your fair share as much as anyone else. If you focus on the positive aspect here—on you RECEIVING an abundance of money, you will be contributing to raising the prosperity consciousness of others, because you are, in effect, volunteering yourself as an example to the world. In this situation, you can say to the world: "Look at me, I wasn't born rich, but I've become prosperous by changing my thinking, and you can do it too." Remember, the money you make goes back into the economy to be distributed to others, which helps prosper everyone you buy from or give money to.

Before you can become rich, you must believe that you deserve it. It's impossible to convince your subconscious mind to bring you money if you have been programmed to the idea that you don't deserve it. We have all heard stories of people who had the ability to make a fortune but lacked the ability to keep it. Such people don't feel worthy of success; they don't think they deserve all that money, so they invariably sabotage themselves when they acquire it.

Sometimes it's not a fear of success but a fear of failure that prevents people from becoming wealthy. A person may be going along well, accumulating money, but then they get sidetracked into a worry loop, thinking to themselves, "I'm making money now, but how long will it last?" "What if I lost it?" "What if people stop buying from me?" "What if the stock market crashes?" "What if I lose my job?" And so on.

Although it's important to be prudent enough to provide for extenuating circumstances, such as a company layoff, we must constantly counteract these negative ideas with positive affirmations such as . . .

"I DESERVE TO BE WEALTHY"

"I DESERVE HAPPINESS," and "I DESERVE SUCCESS."

As soon as you get these thoughts firmly implanted in your consciousness, you have taken a giant step toward achieving wealth.

CHAPTER 5

WORDS

Positive thoughts and words create positive results in any area of your life and when positive thoughts and words are COMBINED with a positive belief, this becomes incredibly powerful and works wonders. Positive thoughts and words are able to create positive results in any area of your life, while defaulting to negative words has the opposite effect. The human mind has the ability to direct the future a bit like a movie director shouting orders when creating a movie. So it can be said that the thoughts that you are thinking are essentially creating the movie of your future experiences. Your thoughts or words will direct your future. And your thoughts will make things happen. So it follows that if you think positive thoughts, you will receive positive results. Your mind listens to your words and thoughts and brings you what you want, just like a magnet attracts iron filings when they come near to the magnetic edges of the magnet.

Be careful what you wish for.
Your mind WILL make your thoughts come true.

Have you ever considered the difference between Willing and Wishing? While the words are sometimes used interchangeably, there is a considerable difference between the two states. Will power contains a powerful emotional component, and while Wishing initially engages your mind in the process of thinking about your desire, Willing adds an emotional component that effectively starts your mind BELIEVING that you can have your desire. Willing is a very powerful way of thinking, and the thoughts that have an enhanced powerful component have the capacity to make greater things happen. Positive verbalizations are a bit like a movie director saying to the future "I want this, I will do this, and they will do that." What many people today seem to forget is that each individual alone has the power to be the author of their very own future life script. No-one else has the power to write your script, although we often defer to those we love, buying into their own fear-based, limiting beliefs. This is where we have the amazing choice—to step into our own power and decide on our own individual future. Do we allow ourselves to be limited by other's beliefs, or do we step out of the shadows and live our best lives? I understand how difficult this process can be, having grown up with a parent who always saw the glass as half empty. But the decision is totally yours—if you want to live your best life, you MUST decide to step up and take control of the scripts that run through your mind every waking hour. And how do you do this? You start by becoming aware of the words you use on a regular basis, and correct yourself when you find yourself slipping into the negative. Once you realize that you're using an inappropriate word, simply stop your sentence and say "Erase" and then replace it with a more empowering word.

For example: "I have SO much that I simply MUST do today . . ." that sentence doesn't feel good at all, just saying it makes me feel so 'put upon' and dragging along in drudgery. Simply re-state the sentence as: "ERASE! I have so many things that I CHOOSE to do today . . ." now this sentence puts me in the powerful drivers seat, so that even if I don't get some of the things done, the intention was there to do it, and I felt empowered in the process of looking at my To Do List. That simple exercise shows the power of changing just ONE word in a sentence to get a much better result.

Use your mental will power.
Make orders in your mind of how you want things to happen.

Positive verbalization power comes from the mind hearing our words or 'hearing' the thoughts in our head, and transmitting

THE POWER OF YOUR MIND!

the orders out into the world, to make them happen. Whether it is getting a dream job or creating a parking space in a busy shopping centre, the relevant orders are transmitted through the body and into the universe with amazing results.

ONE SMALL STEP: Verbally Direct Your Future

Imagine you can positively direct your future like a director shouting directions on a movie. Imagine you are sitting in your car and on the movie screen ahead of you, you can direct what you want to happen. A microphone and a loud speaker in the car will transmit the directions to the world. Take a moment now and verbalize your Top Seven goals. 'Will' your future with your Mind power. Use positive verbalization to 'direct' your future.

"I WILL . . . _____."

"I WILL . . . _____."

"I WILL . . . _____."

Verbalize everything you do and you'll get success in almost everything you do. Verbalize at the start of each day when you write down your goals or think about your goals for the day. Adopt this habit every day, as you shower and prepare for your day, and you will see the level of your success skyrocket. If there is one thing that differentiates a winner from a loser, it would be motivation. The second thing is positive attitude. You either have it or you haven't (and need to get it!) Some people are more positive than others (and some are more negative than others).

Winners simply have a positive attitude.

You need a positive mind to win in business and in life. Your mind impacts your life in two ways. It affects your results AND it affects your perception. A positive mind makes positive things happen and gives you positive results. Not all the time, but most of the time. However, a positive mindset also affects your perception of the events in your world. Having a positive mind is like having positive glasses on! If you have a positive mindset you will spot 'the positives' as they happen during your day and remember them, and you will tend to ignore most of the negative things. However, a negative mindset affects your eyes and is like having negative glasses on. If you have a negative mindset you will focus on the negatives as they happen during your day and remember them and, subsequently, you will ignore most of the positive things.

When it comes to dreams or business opportunities a positive mind will be optimistic and maintain a positive vision. Whereas a negative mind is pessimistic and will create a negative vision. Put these two people on a bare allotment and they will see two different things: Mr Positive sees the potential for flowers, Ms Negative sees the potential for weeds. They've got different glasses on and have a completely different perception of the exact same events! And a negative person won't change their negative glasses until they change their negative mind.

A positive mind is more likely to think positive thoughts. Positive people (with positive minds) are 'lucky' which helps success. Positive people who believe in luck do very well because their mind is on the lookout for 'lucky' opportunities, guiding them to make lucky intuitive decisions and attracting lucky events towards themselves. Your thinking affects your vision. Positive people have a different vision from negative people. Entrepreneurs have a different vision from non-entrepreneurs.

Here are Ten Ways to feed the Positive Aspects of your life:

1. Use positive words, and follow this "Winning Mentality."
2. Surround yourself with positive people; family, friends, teachers, mentors.
3. Find people better than yourself to work with, talk with, and train with.

4. Watch great people. Watch, listen, and learn. In person, on TV, radio or tape.
5. Read inspirational and motivational material; books, stories, and interviews.
6. Listen to uplifting music.
7. Write down a Winner's Checklist first thing in the morning, of things that you need to do during each day to achieve your dreams, and check off your achievements each evening—Make your day a Winner!
8. Relax your mind; a relaxed mind is more positive, creative and productive.
9. Eat healthy food and drink.
10. Have a fit and healthy body—this leads to a fit healthy mind.

Negative thoughts are extremely destructive when you're attempting to maintain a positive approach to living a healthy, wealthy, successful and happy life. Negative thoughts effectively kill your dreams. If you are looking for the best way to be unsuccessful, the secret is to simply start worrying! It works a treat. Negative thoughts are negative orders, which are carried out by the mind like a waiter serving food.

Your future is like a magnet to your thoughts.
If you think negatively before taking action
negative results are almost guaranteed

We all have a negative and a positive voice. But for most people the negative voice is big and loud, like Goliath, while the positive voice is small and quiet, like little David. Your mind hosts a boxing match between these two voices every day. You may be wondering how your negative voice became so loud or how the giant Goliath got to be so big?

Have you ever stopped to actually identify the sources of your negative beliefs and attitudes? Here are some possible sources of your negativity:

- <u>You:</u> Every time you have a negative thought or say a negative word, you are feeding your negative voice in your mind. Every time you have failed at something, you've given your negative voice a banquet to feed on for weeks, months or even years. Have you got a negative thinking job? Health and Safety officers, financial advisors and parents can become exceptionally negative because they are always looking at risks, negatives and worst case scenarios.
- <u>Your Parents:</u> Kids are very demanding. YOU were demanding when you were growing up. Your parents had to say "No" to you many times. So many times, in fact, that it's estimated that you will hear the word 'No' around 100,000 times by the time you hit your late teens.
- <u>Other People:</u> Teachers, friends, relations, shopkeepers have all given you their positive or negative opinion on everything, from the clothes you wear, to the books you read and the food you eat.
- <u>Negative People:</u> Negative people are a dangerous species because their effect is so insidious that you often don't even recognize their influence until it's too late to avoid experiencing the negative results.
- <u>Media:</u> TV, Radio, magazines etc. As a general rule, I would encourage you to avoid anything on TV between 5pm and 7pm. It's highly unlikely to have even the slightest positive effect of the quality of your precious life!
- <u>Stressed mind:</u> By being stressed your mind is less resourceful, less energetic and less positive.
- <u>Unhealthy Food:</u> Eating fatty, sugary and processed unhealthy food has a negative effect on the mind and the body, as does fizzy drinks, coffee and alcohol.
- <u>Stressed (Unfit) Body:</u> Without some activity, exercise and fresh air, the mind does not operate effectively, it operates negatively.

The BBC did a great study as part of the program 'The Human Mind', where they conducted an experiment on two similar people with the intent of measuring the influence external happy or sad stimuli has on a person's mood. They found a set of twins who were almost identical in appearance and personality. The normally inseparable sisters agreed to be separated for a day. Upon waking, one sister was asked to listen to a 'sad' song, then watch a sad emotional film, and finally read a sad 'moving' story. Her identical sister upon waking was asked to listen to uplifting music, then watch a happy film and finally read a 'inspirational' story. Both sisters (still separated) were then taken shopping in a mall. (By watching someone shop, psychologists can accurately observe and track changes in an individual's mood.)

The 'sad' sister went into several shops, saw little that she liked, and in total bought only two items of clothing. In the final shop she visited, she bought a pair of shoes after a long period of uncertainty. Before buying she enquired "If I don't like them, can I bring them back?" (Not a confident comment!) She made her purchase only after repeated reassurances from the shop assistant that she could return the shoes if necessary. The camera crew then followed her as she left the shop and went to be reunited with her sister.

The 'happy' sister eventually appeared, weighed down by 8 bags of clothing! She bounced towards her sister with a big smile on her face and asked how her 'sad' sister had got on. The 'sad' sister replied that she had seen many things she liked, but she had only purchased some shoes. She went into one of her bags to get them out to show her sister. Although she had only just bought them, when she saw them this time, she said, "I don't like them, I'm going to take them back!" In contrast, her happy sister, reflected that she had enjoyed her shopping experience and dived her hand into one of her bags. She removed two identical hats to show her sister, one of which she had bought for her 'sad' sister and she placed it on her head. It was fascinating to see the energy and happiness of the 'happy' sister lifting the mood of her 'sad' sister quickly and transform her facial expression into a smile.

The conclusion from this particular experiment: Music, movies and stories WILL influence your mood. A positive stimulus will put you in a positive mood. Positive music will put you in a positive mood. A positive picture will put you in a positive mood. Positive words will put you in a positive mood. You won't get that from the nightly news! Words and pictures have feelings attached to them. Surround yourself with positive ones.

The previous advice will help you to feed your positive voice and help you to stop feeding your negative giant. But if a negative thought does arrive in your mind there are ways to deal with it. Imagine you are in a car and you have come up with an idea of a destination (dream) to drive towards. If a negative thought arrives, it's like a red traffic light. It's effectively stopping you getting to your dream. When you think a negative thought, imagine a red traffic light and stop the flow of the negative thoughts. Say "STOP!" in your mind. If it's a negative mental movie, say "CUT!" You don't want to keep playing that movie or you will direct your future that way. If you use negative words, you'll get negative results.

If you use weak words you'll get weak results. Here are some weak, non-positive words and some stronger replacements:

WEAK	STRONG
Try	Will do
Nightmare	Interesting
Exhausted	Un-energetic
Problem	Challenge
Forget	Remember
Stressed	Not Calm
Should	Could
Sick	50% Healthy
Weak	Not Strong
Negative	Non-positive
Can't	Can

The word "try" is commonly used in western dialogue, but it's destructive power cannot be overstated. Using this little word is one of the most disempowering traps in our language. The wise Jedi master, Yoda from Star Wars, had it right when he warned . . .

*"You do or you do not
—there is no Try"*

Here are some weak negative phrases and some strong positive alternatives:

NOT POSITIVE	POSITIVE PHRASES
I feel terrible	I'm not feeling great
I'm ill	I'm not feeling 100%

NOT POSITIVE	POSITIVE PHRASES
I'm useless	I'm not brilliant
I'm starving	I'm not fully fuelled up
I'm tired	I'm not very energetic
I've got a problem	I'm still looking for a solution
I've forgotten	I cannot remember yet
I've got bad news	I've got news and it's not nice
I'm useless at that	I'm not brilliant at that . . . yet!
I'll never get to	I could, but have chosen not to
I hate	I am not a lover of
Horrible weather	Not weather for t-shirts
I'll try	I will
I should exercise	I could exercise

No chapter about the power of our Words would be complete without mentioning the huge benefit of Affirmations. In this day and age, I find that people are generally aware about the value of using Affirmations on a regular basis as a means of directing our focus and maximising the law of attraction in our lives. To this end, I have included a list of the Affirmations here, that I have used over the past few years. As I am always on the lookout for new affirmations, I am always collecting them from a variety of sources. So please excuse the lack of acknowledgement of the affirmation sources.

The type of affirmation you choose is a highly personal decision. I would suggest "trying out" affirmations from different sources, to find the type that best suits your unique personality and individual needs, and you can also write your own.

ONE SMALL STEP: Sample Affirmations

- I deserve to be wealthy and prosperous, and this is coming true for me now!
- I am a capable and successful person, and abundance is my birthright.
- I am a powerful, dynamic, and intelligent person, and I am manifesting my abundance now.
- I am self-confident, and my actions are decisive. I attract money to me through my desire to succeed.
- I am entitled to a share of the world's wealth, and this is coming to me now.
- Money knows where I live and she visits me regularly.
- Money is a lover of mine, and I treat her kindly so that she comes to see me more often.
- I am completely relaxed, self-confident, and self-assured in everything I do.
- I can accomplish any goal I desire through planning and self-motivation.
- I have the ability to focus my undivided attention on any particular task at any time. I am able to concentrate deeply on anything I set my mind to. I can shut out all distractions and focus my entire attention on the problem at hand.
- Every problem is an opportunity for me to be creative and I am highly creative. I consider every problem that confronts me as a new door to be opened. I begin every job thinking of new and better ways to accomplish the task.
- I am able to totally relax at will any time I wish. Regardless of the circumstances, I am a very relaxed and calm person, completely in control of myself.

- I have all the energy I need for the day ahead. I am filled with rejuvenating life energy, and my total being is refreshed and energetic.
- I am poised, relaxed, and peaceful. I accept challenges and disagreements with calmness.
- I am abundant in every good way.
- My abundance is making everyone better off.
- I am living a wonderfully inspired and inspiring life.
- I am greeted with love wherever I go.
- I am incredibly powerful right here, right now.
- I have all the skills needed to be a success within me now.
- I love taking inspired action, right here, right now.
- I love to vibrate Wealth and Abundance.
- I am wonderfully supported in my work and home life.
- I experience great love and support from my family and friends.
- I truly love my home and all its contents.
- I love that I get to work everyday in a job that I truly enjoy.
- I love exercising my body and my mind on a daily basis.
- I am now living the most amazingly successful life, in an easy and relaxed manner, in a healthy and positive way.

CHAPTER 6

BELIEFS

Beliefs are incredibly strong thoughts. Your thoughts are the powerhouse that make things happen. Your beliefs can make incredible things happen (like achieving big dreams). Also beliefs can make incredible things happen repeatedly, such as always winning prizes. If you think 'I will win this competition' you are more likely to. If you BELIEVE 'I am lucky' you WILL be lucky. Conversely, if you think 'I am going to catch my son's cold' then you probably will.

Any beliefs you have, actually originated with a thought. So you may ask where did that initial thought come from? There are several possible places to obtain a belief:

- Yourself—you may have just created the thought in your own mind.
- Other People—you may have heard the thought from parents or teachers.
- Education—you may have got it from a book, TV, radio, movie or school.
- Experiences—you may have evolved it following a personal experience during childhood or even in adulthood.

A belief is created by the thoughts that run through your mind on a continuous basis, but it's origin may have been INSPIRED by yourself or someone or something else. Most of your beliefs find evidence to support their existence and this encourages your subconscious mind hold onto them. However we may hold some

.

beliefs in the absence of this supporting evidence, an example of which might be our long-held dreams. We may maintain a belief in our dreams, even in the absence of justifiable proof that we will definitely achieve them. Humans sometimes simply BELIEVE something to be true. For example, some people believe in the Loch Ness Monster, but there is no recent credible proof to support its existence—though this doesn't deter the ardent believers!

Winners don't have to see before they believe it.

Winners believe in their dream and then they achieve their dreams.

Here's an example of the ways in which beliefs influence our present reality:

- Your beliefs will influence how you see the world.
- What you believe, you will achieve, so beliefs can limit or block your success as easily as they can enable your success.
- Conflicting beliefs stop you achieving goals.
- You can create a new belief anytime and get positive results.

Your beliefs and general attitude can influence how you see the world in any particular moment. Our beliefs and attitude are like a pair of glasses though which you see the world. You can choose your beliefs and you can choose your attitude. So it follows that you can choose to wear a pair of positive glasses. If you choose a positive attitude it's like your mind tends to search for the positives in your environment, kind of like playing the card game 'Snap'. Once you adopt your positive attitude, your mind will search for the positives around you, and you will consciously notice all the positive events, while your mind ignores or even hides many of the negative items and experiences that cross your path in the same period of time.

ONE SMALL STEP:—Identify Your Beliefs

What you truly believe, you WILL ultimately achieve. So let's look more closely at your beliefs. Have you ever stopped to consider what it is that you believe about specific aspects of your life? Chances are that this is not something you engage in on a regular basis . . . and you're not alone! Most of the population take their beliefs for granted, and never even consider the active role they take in belief creation. Take a moment now to write down whatever you think that you believe. Record whatever comes to mind immediately (don't sensor yourself) and write down as much as you can. What do you believe? Complete the statement as fully and quickly as possible:

"I believe . . . _____"

"I believe . . . _____"

"I believe . . . _____"

"I believe . . . _____"

"I believe . . . _____"

"I believe . . . _____"

"I believe . . . _____"

"I believe . . . _____"

"I believe . . . _____"

Make sure you have written any beliefs related to work, family, friends, love, health, happiness, success, money, luck, winning, dreams and rich, successful and famous people. If not, write down a statement about each. What do you believe?

When you've completed your list, take a look to see which negative beliefs are giving you negative results. Which beliefs might be holding you back? Now put a line through any which are stopping you from being successful and winning. You need to 'cut' negative beliefs from your potential future. As you draw the line, say 'Cut' out loud to reinforce your intention to remove this belief from your repertoire.

The aim now is to destroy your negative beliefs and replace them with new positive, empowering beliefs! Out with the old, in with the new. Doesn't that feel great to say that? You CAN create a new belief the same way you acquired your old beliefs, with a simple thought. The last time you had a new belief/thought was because you:

- Witnessed or had an experience which INSPIRED you to form the thought
- Discovered information which made you think the new thought
- Just had the random thought

We can use the latter route to create a new belief. The process is like creating a mantra. A mantra is a sentence or affirmation that you repeat over and over to strengthen your sense of belief, while a belief is just a thought that has been reinforced and empowered with emotion.

ONE SMALL STEP:—New Mantras Build New Beliefs

Think about your number one dream goal. Picture yourself succeeding in a particular task or activity, or in life in general (over a period of 1, 2, 5 or 10 years). How would you describe yourself? Write the words that come to mind down now.

_____

_____

_____

_____

_____

_____

How will you feel when you achieve a particular goal? Write the feeling words that come to mind (try to be as VIVID in your description as possible):

_____

_____

_____

_____

_____

_____

OK now write the words "I am . . ." below and choose words from the above list to include after it. For example: "I am a lucky, happy, winner" or "I am a magnificent money magnet."

"I am _____"

"I am _____"

"I am _____"

"I am _____"

"I am _____ "

"I am _____ "

"I am _____ "

Think about your other Six goals and picture yourself achieving those goals. How would you describe yourself? Record the words that come to mind now.

_____
_____
_____
_____
_____
_____
_____

How will you FEEL when you achieve your goal? Write the feeling words that come to mind down—the more VIVID the experience, the more effective the exercise will be. If you're building dreams, why not build JUICY dreams that are BUZZING with energy!!!!

_____
_____
_____
_____
_____
_____

Have a look at those words and your first mantra, and consider if they are much different. The above words can be added to your first mantra or you can create a second mantra by writing the words "I am . . ." in front of them. Put effort into one goal and one mantra every day. Say it several times. I suggest you focus your biggest effort on your dream goal initially. When you want to make another of your goals a priority for a month, then rotate your attention so you put more effort into the associated mantra.

Focus on the goal directly in front of you on a day-to-day basis and think of your dream on a week-to-week basis. Imagine you are walking towards your goal, climbing the side of a large mountain. Acknowledge that some steps are easy and some steps are hard. Some steps require a leap or a bridge to cross the gap between not having and having achieved your goal. Each step takes you closer to your goal and each one is a test of your strength, stamina, courage and determination. Keep your focus on the next step, instead of letting your mind wander to all the challenges that lay ahead of you in your journey. By all means visualize the big goal, but always bring your focus back to the step in front of you.

How do you WANT to feel? Think about your big Seven Goals. Imagine you have achieved them all. How will you FEEL? (Always come back to anchor yourself to the FEELING that you desire—that is your power source in this process).

_____
_____
_____
_____
_____
_____
_____

A very good question to ask yourself at this point is "What is stopping you from feeling that right NOW?"

_____
_____
_____
_____
_____
_____
_____

Remember you choose your thoughts, you choose how you want to feel. Be happy now, don't wait until you get your goal. By using 'feeling' words your mind will focus on these feelings and give you those feelings now. It also gives your mind a 'feeling' goal. You can change or add to your mantra at any time, but you really need to discipline yourself to get into the habit of using it on a regular basis.

CHAPTER 7

MINDSET

A person who approaches each day with a confident mindset will invariably produce a confident performance. Therefore, a positive mind means a positive performance. Our mood reflects what's happening within our mind. As shown in previous chapters, a lot of external stimulus, like what we hear, read and see, affects our mind and our mood, because this external stimuli influences our internal thoughts. However, we CHOOSE our thoughts. The three positive techniques covered so far that are very effective in creating a positive mindset are:

- Positive Visualization (Creating a Mental Movie)
- Positive Language (Writing and Directing Your Movie Script)
- Positive Beliefs and Self Esteem (Creating Mantras and Affirmations)

Positive thoughts create a positive mind. I include positive mental pictures in the term positive thoughts, because if you think positive, you will invariably feel more positive, and research has shown that most people dominantly think in pictures rather than words.

Another route which helps to create a positive mind is through the utilization of positive body language. Your mind is closely connected to your body in many ways. As part of your minds' innate survival mechanism, your mind will monitor your body position and facial expression looking for confidence or concern.

If it detects a 'concerned' face or body, it will initiate a stress response to prepare the body for battle! If your mind detects a confident face or body, it relaxes, creating a confident mind and an overall feeling of confidence throughout the body. Essentially, any motion creates E-motion.

Positive body language creates and reinforces the use of positive language in the thoughts we think. If you can read someone's body you can usually get a pretty good idea of what they are thinking. It follows that if you don't feel confident, then you will find it difficult to look confident. The best way to look confident (on the outside) is to feel confident (on the inside). Using more confident body language will help you feel more confident and look more confident. Therefore, the best way to APPEAR and BE confident externally is to FEEL confident internally. Acting positively on the outside is not as potent as feeling positive on the inside, but it can be used as a trigger to encourage more positive feelings of confidence on the inside. If you walk confidently, you will feel confident. If you act rushed, you will find that you end up feeling rushed. Conversely, if you walk calmly, you will feel calmer internally, if you act scared, you will feel scared. If you start dancing, you will start feeling good and improve your mood.

It is widely recognized that manipulating body position has a direct influence on the experience of emotions. For example, standing up while making telephone calls improves confidence. The body's position is linked to the mind's emotion. If you lie down, you will calm down. If you stand up, you will feel confident. If you're head is down, your confidence will go down. Keep your chin up, and you keep your confidence up. If you cross your arms, you become defensive, negative and retain less information. If you smile, you will feel more relaxed, positive and happy. If you frown, you will feel stressed and nervous. If we act positive, we feel more positive. If we think positive, we also feel positive.

The moment we create a positive mental movie, use positive directing or repeat a positive mantra, we actually 'switch' our mind to a positive confident mood. Using any one of these three techniques creates confidence and produces great results and performances. As stated previously, visualization can be considered a SUPER POWER, an extremely potent tool to use to boost mental state and subsequently achieve a better physical performance, especially when combined with positive beliefs. Combining these two power-packed processes will ensure an amazing performance. The "Switch" technique, which I shall explain later in this chapter, powerfully combines both of these elements, with the bonus of engaging your imagination to create a peak state prior to completing an action. You may be surprised to discover you have already used this very powerful technique when you were a kid.

Pretending to be or do something new, is a very powerful pass-time that we tend to discredit when we reach adulthood, however, by pretending to be someone who you perceive to be powerful and skillful, you not only become full of confidence and self-belief (because you are acting like your hero, not yourself) but you may actually adopt some of your hero's traits, just by pretending to be them. When you're copying them, you are learning to behave like them, and this is actually one of the the fastest ways to learn a set of skills! This "pretending" technique is sometimes referred to as Modeling. Acting or pretending is very similar to modeling, however, 'Modeling' can be approached in a more deliberate and methodical way to achieve more specific performance results. Utilizing this technique, you identify what skills or characteristics a hero has and then imagine you have them too! Effectively, you begin to ACT like them. Who wouldn't want to take the 'direct' route to the top, rather than fiddling around at the base of the mountain wondering if you even have the skills to actually get to the top of the mountain? One word of warning: taking the "short cut" is only appropriate in certain circumstances—there are many times when you really need to take your time and learn skill sets completely and thoroughly, to ensure your own safety and that of others . . . I think intuitively, you will KNOW when the quick route is appropriate and when you need to take your time and do your due diligence. Make sure you act responsibly and follow your own inner knowing in these cases.

If another human can do it, you can do it.

If no other human has done it (yet), IMAGINE you can do it, and you CAN do it.

Imagination and visualization help you achieve great things.

Think of a person you admire who's performance in some area you would like to emulate. How do you suppose they act and think? What do you think are their favorite mottos and quotes? What are the particular skills and characteristics they exhibit that you want to copy? Use your imagination to act, think and feel like the person. The person can be real, fictional, alive or dead. You can act, copy, and pretend to be anyone. If you need to build your confidence, ACT like someone who is brimming with confidence. If you fake it at first, you will eventually make it. You can model someone just by watching them or reading about them or speaking to them in person (or on the phone!). Use your imagination and then go do it!

Identify qualities that one or more of your heroes have that you need to copy to succeed. Record those qualities here:

_____

_____

_____

_____

_____

Complete a SWOT analysis (identify your Strengths, Weaknesses, any Opportunities, & Threats to your success) and identify what skills you will need to acquire to succeed in your efforts:

_____

_____

_____
_____
_____

One essential quality of any business or sporting hero is having the courage to take ACTION. Every hero needs to be brave to take risks and follow their dreams. You will need to be brave too if you are to follow your own dream. To apply the concept of 'Modeling' to improve your performance, imagine you are sitting in the drivers seat of your car, and picture a big red switch on the dash-board, next to the steering wheel. When you feel under pressure and feel that you need the extra boost of your adrenaline from your secret 'Hero Ability' to be added to your skill set, press the big red 'Hero Switch'. The qualities of your hero that you identified above, will magically be bestowed upon you and your confidence and your performance will henceforth skyrocket! (Isn't this the COOLEST game?)

ONE SMALL STEP: Create a Mental Movie of Your Dream

Think of your dream goal. Imagine you have already achieved it. As you visualize this 'mental movie' of yourself in the future, what SINGLE WORD would you use to describe yourself?

- How do you FEEL?
- How would you ACT?
- What THOUGHTS are going through your mind?

_____
_____
_____
_____
_____
_____
_____
_____
_____

Now it is time to start thinking and acting AS IF you have already achieved your dream. You can switch into this state of mind any time you want. Imagine you are your 'I am a Hero' future self every day, and imagine the advice you get and the actions you tell yourself you MUST take to achieve your dreams.

Listen to your own advice and take those actions!

The technique above does not require you to act like one of your heroes per se (you don't need to be jumping tall buildings in a single stride), but for you to ACT like YOU ARE THE HERO NOW! It is important that you understand that you ALREADY HAVE all you need within you right now, in this very moment, to be the hero of your own life, and that you don't need to wait until tomorrow, or next week or next year to get into the game. That is exactly how successful people like Mohammed Ali thought and acted when he stated "I am the greatest" years before he actually got there. As a small computer company, Hewlett Packard founders said they 'acted like a big company' in the way they spent their time and money and made decisions, because they believed that one day they would be. It worked! Act like a big company. Act like you ARE the greatest now.

You can be whoever you want to be.
You can choose to be the bravest, greatest, happiest, most successful and the most positive person in your world . . . Every Day!!

Being successful or being a 'winner' in business could be evaluated in many different ways. One obvious way to find a business winner is to look for millionaire entrepreneurs. A survey of Britain's estimated 5,000 self made millionaires by Tulip Financial Research, found that millionaires have seven common traits:

- Take risks
- Never switch off
- Not afraid to fail and keep going regardless
- Think laterally
- Believe that they will be successful

- Break the rules
- Are driven and determined.

The traits of a millionaire are similar to the traits required to be a winner in sport. Have a look at the following list, and see if you can model any of these characteristics to achieve your dream:

- Hard work
- Honest and trustworthy
- Get along with people easily
- Enjoy work
- Take opportunities
- Enjoy being your own boss
- Intelligence
- Being disciplined and dedicated to success
- Being physically fit and healthy
- Employ good people (attract good people in general)
- Have a supportive partner

These are the thoughts and habits of winners and you can model them! The best way to become a success in sport or business is to DO IT! Not study it. "Doing" is the greatest teacher. Learning from and modeling a hero is one of the best ways to learn to be a hero oneself. You don't just learn HOW to do something; you learn how to be GREAT at it! That is one of the reasons this chapter is so important. The second reason is imagining you are a hero is amazingly powerful. Imagination is sometimes more important than knowledge.

THE HERO SWITCH

Write a list now of who your heroes are. The list may include a person you have admired for years or one you have admired for just a few minutes:

_____

_____

_____
_____
_____
_____
_____
_____
_____
_____
_____
_____
_____
_____
_____
_____
_____
_____
_____
_____
_____
_____
_____
_____
_____

Add to this list every time you find a new hero and then decide on a specific date by which you would like to meet your hero in some form. You will be surprised at the influence this has on your life. You are only as successful as the people you meet, know, hang around and admire. Be aware of that. Improve your list of contacts. Friends and heroes and you will improve your life. Fly like an eagle.

> _"You will be the same person in five years as you are today—_
> _apart from the people you meet and the books that you read."_
> _~ Charlie 'Tremendous' Jones ~_

ONE SMALL STEP: Relive Your Positive Past

Think of a time when you were really confident, positive, and 'in the zone.' Take yourself back to that experience. Remember how you looked, felt, and talked. Answer the following five questions and note the first answer that comes to mind and trust it:

- What word comes to mind to describe how you felt? (This is your Power Word):

  _____

- What color do you associate with that experience?

  _____

- What sound do you associate with that experience?

  _____

- What texture or feeling do your associate with that experience?

  _____

- Which sense is strongest for you, the color, sound, or feeling?

  _____

CREATE YOUR OWN POSITIVE BUBBLE

Now imagine that every time you say your 'Power Word', you switch on the positive bubble and you hear the sound, see the color or feel the feeling. Imagine you are surrounded by a bubble filled with that color, with that feeling or that sound around you. Imagine the bubble is bullet proof so any non-positive comments, thoughts and energies simply bounce off it.

The 'Hero Switch' and 'Positive Bubble' are powerful techniques to use while you are experiencing a broad variety of real life situations. Both will encourage you to adopt a more positive mindset which, in turn, will be more likely to result in a positive performance. When combined with the other previously mentioned tools (the mental movie, directing and the mantra), they make for a winning toolkit! The latter three tools are best used in preparation for a brilliant physical performance. In endurance and 'stop start' sports like golf or football, these tools can be used during the performance as well as preceding the activity. In a business setting, they can be effectively implemented during a working day, before each meeting, phone call or specific activities faced throughout the day.

My first question for any person who is struggling with poor performance when they have experienced major success in the past is always "What were you THINKING when you were produced successful results in the past?" Whatever their reply is, my response is always to encourage them to start thinking the same thoughts that they were thinking when they were winning, and they will regain their winning form. My second question for any person who has had major success is "What were you DOING with your body (position-wise) when you were successful?" Whatever their reply, my response is always "Start doing that again and you will start winning again!" Great preparation always produces great performances, so prepare yourself for success by assuming the posture or your winning self! This appears to be a very simple trigger, but it has proven to be extremely effective in attracting excellent results, so use these physical anchors to trigger your winning performance once again.

Pretending is also a deceptively simple yet extremely powerful activity, so it pays to make the effort and fully engage your imagination. Identify the emotion you want to feel, engage your imagination and you WILL enter the emotional state of a winner. Imagine you are confidently talking with friends. When you need to speak to someone and you are resisting connecting with them, take a moment to imagine you are fully engaged in an enjoyable conversation with them and you are feeling confident and relaxed. This type of mental rehearsal will pre-pave you for success when you do actually have the conversation in real life. Think back to a time when you were really happy on a special occasion. Then the next time you are feeling a little sad or flat and want to boost your mood, imagine you are back at that event or day and experience those happy feelings once more! Engage those happy vibes. When you make the call, if you have activated those happy memories, at least you will be showing up as a happy individual, so the conversation is more likely to take on that happy tone.

When you want to be confident in a certain situation, then imagine you are in a situation where you are relaxed and confident. If you are engaged in a competition and you're in a winning position, imagine the scores are level or even you are behind on the scoreboard, although this seems a little counter-intuitive, it will help you to stay relaxed and allow you to release some of the pressure to succeed. You are usually the first person to recognize when you are performing at your best, so replay that situation in your imagination. For difficult situations, imagine easy situations, when losing, imagine you are winning etc. For business presentations, imagine talking to family, for cold calls, imagine calling friends and so forth. These little mental switches are great for controlling the amount of pressure to perform that you experience at any given time, allowing you to increase or decrease the pressure to encourage a peak performance in any given situation.

If you want to boost your motivation in a certain area, you can imagine you're in a situation that will increase your level of motivation and hunger to perform well. You know in your heart what motivates you to take action, and if you are still unsure, then simply imagine that you DO know exactly what you have to do to get into action. In this scenario, the feelings and emotions behind the words you say to yourself are as important as the words themselves. Whether your primary emotion is confidence or anger, positive or negative, it may assist you to boost your confidence in the face of fear. A painful or negative experience or emotion can be as powerful a motivator as the most positive experience.

The 'switch' technique can be used with a physical 'prop' or anchor, commonly called a 'trigger'. Have you ever had an occasion when you came across a picture, a distinctive smell, a song or location and it immediately brought back memories of a past experience? The smell or song was, in effect, a trigger. We can deliberately switch ourselves into a certain mood if we use the same trigger 'switch' every time. We can use an aural, visual or kinesthetic switch. Music can be a powerful 'switch' to change your mood. Select some music that you associate with the emotion you want to create. For example, music that makes you feel happy and confident. Play this music every time you want to increase this emotion and the 'switch' will become strong and powerful. Play the same track before you perform and observe the difference in your performance. Have a track you listen to when you wake up and take a shower. Before bed, slow the music down and turn down the volume. Classical music is very effective for relaxing or creative thinking. Personally, my Ipod is loaded with several types of playlists—a 'Power Up' playlist which I use when I want to get my heart rate up and boost my emotions, a 'Chill' playlist for when I choose to calm down and relax and a 'Genius' play list of instrumental music that gets my creative juices flowing.

Think about the last time you felt the particular emotion you want to stimulate, like confidence. Put yourself back in that memory. What picture, color, and visual image have you created? Think of this image, color or place when you want to 'switch' to that state. It could be a location, picture or color. This is called a Visual Switch.

The third tool, called a Kinesthetic switch, is about creating a 'body switch' either in the position of the body, the clothes on the body, or a particular feeling experienced in your body. You can perform a specific movement with your body before you think of that memory, for example, clasping your hands together, tapping your head, pinch your arm. You can use a verbal statement simultaneously, such as tapping your leg and say or think "I am calm" or tap your head and say "I am a wonderful winner!" I have a Kinesthetic Switch that I use on daily basis—whenever I achieve something good or great, I close my right hand into a fist, pump it once or twice and say "Yes". While you may think that that is a pretty pointless habit, I have found that if you do it regularly and with emotion, those emotions actually accumulate (called 'Stacking'). The effect of this is that I can be in a neutral state, not feeling particularly pumped or negative, just flat-lining, and if I pump my fist a few of times and say "Yes!" I can actually feel my mood lifting and my heart rate increases. That, for me, is a really important skill to have. Isn't that why you're reading this book—to gain more control over your thoughts and feelings?

Another method of utilizing the Kinesthetic Switch is by wearing the same clothing for specific performances. If you experience success wearing a certain type of clothing, then this sometimes forms a link in your subconscious mind with being successful (think of the common habits that sportsmen create, such as wearing "lucky socks or jocks" etc.) From a more general perspective, it is common knowledge that the clothes you wear affect your mindset and your mood. The style and color of your clothing and what you use them for are very significant to your mind and mood. Your mind and body build up a strong association with clothes. So casual style clothing should not be used for competing in a running race because you link a different type of energy and behavior to being on the beach than you do when you are running a race. When you are cooking, put on an apron and you'll change into your "Cooking expert" mode and get better results! When working, wear work clothes and change when you finish work, in order to separate the time mentally (this is especially important for those who work from home.) Whatever clothes you choose, dress like the person you want to BECOME. Dress like success and be aware of the impression you are making. Imagine you were a complete stranger looking at yourself, what would you think?

ONE SMALL STEP: Access Your Own Power Hand

This technique is similar to the Bubble Exercise and uses your memory of a past experience to influence a current or future event in a positive manner. It is a powerful way to create a positive state of mind and can be used to overcome challenges and fears. Think of a time when you felt confident, calm and happy. Put yourself back in that experience. Remember how you looked, felt, thought, and talked. Now write the first answers that come to mind to the following questions:

How would you describe yourself?

_____
_____
_____
_____
_____

Now imagine the memory is in your hand. Look down at your hand. What color do you see and associate with that experience?

_____
_____
_____
_____
_____

Now put your hand up to your ear. What sound do you hear and associate with that experience?

_____
_____
_____
_____

Now look down at your hand. What texture or feeling do you feel and associate with that experience?

_____
_____
_____

Now you have created a "Power Hand", which will fill you will confidence. Use it anytime you need it, especially before an important event or facing a fear. You can choose your thoughts and you can choose you body language. Positive body language sends a signal to the mind that you are moving confidently so it makes your mind feel more confident. Get someone who is sad or crying to look up at the sky and watch the difference in their mood! Someone who is thinking positive thoughts will look positive and confident. Someone using positive body language will feel positive and confident. Our mind and emotions are always affected by our body position. Choose positive body language. It's one of the reasons the 'Act As If' technique works so well. If you keep your head up and walk tall, your confident body language is spotted by the mind and which in turn, makes you feel more confident.

Are you walking like a winner or a loser?
If you are going to become a pro you've got to walk like a pro.
If you act like a pro, you will start thinking like a pro.
But you have got to practice, prepare, eat and dress like a pro too!
The same goes for becoming World Class, a Millionaire or a CEO.

You can use either of the two 'hero switch' methods and modeling to inspire a successful performance! Combine it with a positive mental movie and positive directing, and you will be amazed at your performance. It only takes a few moments to do, but it's worth it! Using your Hero Mantra or your Hero Switch, will boost the positive focus of your mind if you use it before, during or after your performance. Psych yourself up! The alternative option is to rush into your performance unprepared, and receive a second-rate result!

Elite sportspeople think and feel in specific ways to achieve outstanding physical performances. The challenge here is for you to model successful athletes, to learn how to think the same winning thoughts and adopt the same feelings that they think and feel, to upgrade any of your negative thought patterns and non-constructive feelings. Then you will more than likely see significant improvements in the quality of your thoughts and subsequently enhance your performance results in virtually any area of your life.

Your performance is profoundly influenced by your thinking—by the things you imagine and the statements you whisper to yourself. Thoughts are powerful—thoughts actually MAKE things happen. Thoughts are the building blocks from which you create your beliefs, attitudes, behaviors, and every aspect of your performance in life. Every thought you have affects you in some way, either empowering or limiting you. There are no 'neutral' thoughts. Yet few people recognize the enormous power of their moment to moment thinking, and fewer still actually use this awareness in their daily life. Every performance starts in your mind. The best performances occur when you take control of your thinking. Champions give themselves a mental edge by standing guard at the door of their mind—by taking control of their thinking, and by deliberately choosing to focus on the positive.

Everyone knows they're supposed to 'be positive'—to think positively, and to discourage negativity. Yet for many people, thoughts just seem to 'happen' before they know about it! When you hear people claiming "I can't help it. I do it automatically!" You need to know that that excuse is just a cop out—a way of avoiding taking responsibility for their actions and their results. Thoughts don't 'just happen' to you—YOU THINK THEM! There is an ACTIVE process requiring both CHOICE and ACTION. There can be no escaping the fact that you CHOOSE your thoughts—how else could they get there? Yet even knowing this, some people still indulge in negative thinking and problem focusing—rather than looking for solutions and always expecting the best for themselves. Part of the problem is, of course, that negative thinking has become a habit—not only for individuals, but for the society in general. Like any habit, it takes EFFORT and a WILLINGNESS to change. So the issue for many people is that they need to be personally convinced of the detriment of negative thinking on their performance and in their lives, and of the enormous advantages available to those who continually focus on positive thoughts that are filled with possibility.

However important thoughts may be in the achievement of success in life, feelings are equally as important. Your performance at work; in your relationships; in education; in sport; in fact, in every area of your life, is profoundly influenced by your feelings. How you FEEL affects how well you PERFORM. Your emotional states influence your thinking, your behavior, your tone of voice, your posture, and even your health. But, like thoughts, feelings don't 'just happen' to you—feelings are CHOICES. Champions recognize this and choose feelings that empower them, thus enabling them to fully utilize their physical prowess and mental skills. Winners have learned how to actively choose the states they live in.

How many good feelings do you have right now? And how much time in a day do you spend feeling good? Likewise, how many bad feelings can you identify . . . . and how much time do you spend in a day feeling bad? Think about it for a minute. If you're like a lot of people, you will probably only be able to think of a few good feelings—but lots of bad ones! For instance, a short list of bad feelings might run like this: Worried; Depressed; Sad; Frustrated; Unconfident; Uptight; Angry; Tired; Tense; Bad; Embarrassed; Pressured; Jealous; Anxious; Unmotivated; Lonely; Weak; Victimized; Sorry-for-self; Nervous; Powerless; Self righteous; Apathetic; Trapped; Unloved; Pitiful; Heavy; Procrastinating; Lousy; Vindictive; Down; Put-upon; Rushed; Sick; Tentative; Bashful; Grumpy; Hesitant; Confused; Stressed; Uncertain; Uncreative; Pensive; Lost; Betrayed; Itchy; Spaced-out; In Crisis; Directionless; Stuck; Impatient; Hurt; Unprepared; Clumsy; Bored; Sullen; Slow; Fragile; Un-coordinated; Guilty; Greedy; Anguished; Fearful; Selfish; Regretful; Grieving; Isolated; Withdrawn; and Sleepy . . . . to name just a few!

What do champions feel? How do they use their emotional states to generate excellence in themselves? What winning feelings do they choose? I've listed some below that I've identified in peak performers. Perhaps you can think of others. Why not choose, right now, to experience one of the following champion feelings:

- JOYFUL—a feeling of intense happiness
- ENTHUSIASTIC—a feeling of being fully alive and energized
- PURPOSEFUL—a feeling of certainty and direction in your life
- DETERMINED—a feeling of being fully committed to a task or goal
- COURAGEOUS—a feeling of strength in the face of adversity or risk
- FOCUSED—a feeling of pinpoint concentration
- LOVED and LOVING—a feeling of caring, and giving of yourself
- ADVENTUROUS—a feeling of excitement and challenge
- MOMENTUM—a feeling of moving to a destination
- BELONGING—a feeling of connection to others
- TIMING—a feeling of being in perfect sync with outside forces
- FLOW—a sense of being divinely guided and being in sync with the world.

Every instant, you're creating or manufacturing some kind of feeling—whether it be a negative feeling like indifference, anger, sullenness, apathy or lacking confidence; or a positive feeling like joy, confidence, enthusiasm, excitement, conviction, or some of the others listed above.

The trouble is, that many people simply don't recognize, or label, their feeling states. As a consequence, their behavior is being directed unconsciously—by feelings they are not even aware of! Because your behavior is profoundly affected by your feelings, if you don't really know or are aware of what you're feeling—how can you be in charge of your behavior, or your performances? In order to be in charge of your personal performance, you want to be aware of your feeling states, and maintain that awareness from moment to moment.

Take a moment, right now, and recognize what you're feeling—right now, right this instant! What are you feeling, right now, as you read this article? Don't dismiss the question, or dodge the answer by saying "I'm feeling OK" or "all right", or "nothing", or "I don't know". Find out! Get in touch with yourself, with your feelings, and describe what you're currently experiencing. Put a label on your feelings.

_____

_____

_____

_____

_____

_____

_____

_____

_____

It's important to LABEL your feelings. If you don't put labels on them you'll find them difficult to change (if they're negative), and you also won't understand what is directing your behaviors! Once you've identified a feeling or emotional state, then you can go about changing it if it is disempowering or counter-productive. In addition, if it's a positive and useful feeling or emotional state, then you can actively enhance and AMPLIFY it, making it even MORE effective and powerful in your life.

It's incredibly important to have a vocabulary of champion feelings—because if you can't conceptualize or put a name to a feeling, how can you ever experience it? If you don't identify a feeling, then you won't ever feel it—or understand what it is that you're feeling, and how to use it. If a feeling is not in your language, then you won't make use of it in your life. Why impoverish yourself by limiting your range of positive emotions to just a few? Practice EXPERIENCING champion feelings, and USE them in your life.

The subconscious mind is an amazing part of our humanity that manages and controls our entire being. It shapes behavior, identity, and beliefs. It allows us to form a relationship with other people to fulfill our goals and dreams. In other words, the subconscious mind allows us to use extraordinary powers and create whatever we desire. Although the exact scope and abilities of the subconscious mind have not yet been discovered, it is my belief that by harnessing this unique internal "computer", we can create an AMAZING life and achieve true happiness. Everything BEGINS with a thought, the primary signal that goes into our subconscious minds. Our thoughts are what guides and commands our subconscious mind.

ONE SMALL STEP: TRANSFORMING YOUR SET OF BELIEFS

By transforming from within, you can change your thoughts and set of beliefs to acquire a new identity, ultimately achieving a new world of self-confidence, health, happiness, and peace. This is how you lay the groundwork for a new life—how you think and, by thinking, you can create anything you desire. You can build strong relationships with people and become a powerhouse of success in all aspects of your life. Everything begins with a thought. A thought is the first step toward any accomplishment. If we enthusiastically think about knowledge, wealth, health, peace, and spirituality, we will become knowledgeable, wealthy, healthy, and peaceful and become successful in this world as well as the hereafter. This success will come to those who are able to think this way.

The reason why so many people find it difficult to THINK AND CREATE is because in principle, the phenomenon of thought is not an independent component within us by which we can, at any moment, create thoughts that are positive, creative, goal-oriented, constructive, inspiring, and productive, Rather, thought is generated from a person's belief system. Therefore, we must first change the QUALITY of our thoughts. Wealthy people have grand and wealth-generating beliefs. With a strong sense of self confidence they PURSUE wealth, and—with their positive beliefs—they ATTAIN that which they desire. Students who get accepted into great schools believe strongly in themselves; the thoughts generated from their belief drive them to constantly work hard and take positive steps forward, resulting in their acceptance. People who win competitions first see themselves as winners in their mind's eye—and so they win. The law of life is the law of beliefs.

From the moment people are born, a system begins to take shape inside them—their "belief system." This means that all the information that is gathered through their five senses and every thought that goes through their head is processed by their subconscious and turned into a belief. All of the elements of your environment, including media, such as the internet, radio and television, and especially the people who surround you daily—your parents, teachers, friends and other family members—are all architects building, shaping, and structuring your belief system. Let's say that during your childhood, your math teacher praises you in front of the class for correctly solving a problem. You will begin to believe in your mathematical abilities, and when you come across a math problem, you'll solve it. Why? Because your ABILITIES are determined by your BELIEFS. In other words, this kind of belief creates a powerful notion inside you, which guides you toward solving the problem. Beliefs even play an important role in building ones' morale. A strong belief in yourself builds confidence, and a weak belief creates uncertainty for achieving success. What you believe in is what you create. Your achievements in life are built by your beliefs. This, here, is where the role of the subconscious, which is responsible for building a person's beliefs, becomes clear.

Another important factor that plays an essential role in the quality of our thoughts is our MORALE. Good morale creates positive, hopeful, and creative thoughts. On the other hand, a withering, depressed, and dejected morale creates negative, destructive and toxic thoughts. In addition to beliefs, morale is also a necessary ingredient in the thought process; both must be present and working together to create a thought. Let's imagine that your thoughts are a bird flying with two wings. One wing is powered by your general belief system, which has been shaped from your birth up until now. The other wing is your morale and the quality of your feelings, which determines where your bird (in this case, your thoughts) will fly and on which branch it will perch after soaring through the sky of your life. The bird that is tired, possessing a discouraged morale and, at the same time, with no positive and character-forming beliefs, always flies with two broken wings; it perches on ruins and broken walls, taking the owner of those thoughts to the brink of destruction. You may now be asking, "Well what is it inside us that creates these two wings? What is the phenomenon that creates belief and morale inside us?" It is essentially our subconscious mind that generates our belief and morale. Once you become aware of your subconscious mind and take hold of its powerful reins, you too can always create the best beliefs and the most uplifted morale within you. You can equip your bird of thought with two strong wings and by using them, build and enjoy the best life possible. Everything begins with a thought and that thought is where transformation begins. We ARE what we believe. If people are after success, happiness, and joy in their lives, they must know that they can achieve great things and embrace true happiness only by thinking the right kind of positive, creative and goal-oriented thoughts.

The single most important difference between individuals is the difference in their belief system. In fact, the overall success, happiness and wealth of each country is determined by the collective beliefs of its people. Our beliefs are constructed by our subconscious mind, and the subconscious mind is like a computer whose primary source of input is the information it receives through the five senses, as well as any strand of thought that the subconscious focuses on for an extended period of time. Effectively the subconscious mind processes these pieces of information to create our belief system.

If people want to change their thoughts and way of thinking,
They must create change in their belief systems.
You can change your belief system by sending
appropriate signals to your subconscious mind.

We should always be aware of ourselves and the kinds of signals we receive through our five senses and through our thoughts. This ensures that in a constant state of self-awareness, we send the best possible signals to our subconscious mind.

When you think positively and see the beauty in the world, listen to uplifting music, reflect on inspiring affirmations, smell a lovely fragrance, or enjoy eating a delicious meal, these positive signals enter your subconscious mind and, in addition to creating a wonderful mental outlook, have a great effect within you and even on the world outside you. The reflection of these beautiful things will come back to you and make your life more and more the life you desire it to be. The other parameter that distinguishes mental signals is their intensity or power. The stronger the intensity of the signals that enter your subconscious, the more of an effect they can have on it. For example, when you ask, "Why am I successful?" this signals holds a specific strength, but when you associate the matter with a higher spiritual being and say, "How is it that you have made me so successful?" this sentence transmits a stronger signal to your subconscious mind and will ultimately have a greater effect.

By embracing a spiritual approach to life, you create a divine feeling inside you, which allows your subconscious mind to produce wonderful beliefs and helps you achieve your desired goals. When you call on God or the Universe for something, you must BELIEVE that what you asked for is right behind the door, just waiting for you to take it. In fact, when you ask for something, your faith is a factor that increases the intensity of the signal that enters the subconscious, helping you reach your goal sooner.

CHAPTER 8

LIVING THE LAW OF ATTRACTION

Ever since the release of the phenomenally successful book and TV movie 'The Secret', people everywhere are asking how they can make the Law of Attraction work. Most people have found themselves feeling that it isn't as easy as they thought it would be and they can't figure out WHY the Law of Attraction works for some and not for all. Here's the truth . . . . The Law of Attraction is ALWAYS working, whether you realize it or not. The question isn't IF the Law of Attraction is working. The real question is if the Law of Attraction is working FOR you or AGAINST you?

There are five steps the in Law of Attraction process and whether you are attracting what you want or what you don't want, I guarantee you are, either consciously or subconsciously, already using these 5 steps:

- Decide What You Want.
- Visualize in GREAT Detail.
- Remove any Resistance You May Hold Towards Your Desires.
- Take Inspired ACTION.
- RELEASE all Attachment to your Desire.

You may have heard all this a million times over, and yet if you are like most people, it seems like the Law of Attraction STILL doesn't work. Well now I'm here telling you that it IS working—it just isn't working FOR you! So what's the deal? The deal is that the Law of Attraction is deceptively simple . . . you get what you spend the majority of your time focusing on. This said, I guarantee that you are ALWAYS ATTRACTING what you are focusing on.

ONE SMALL STEP: Where Are You Now?

- WHAT'S YOUR LIFE LIKE RIGHT NOW? Grab a pen and ink your answer. Describe your life in DETAIL . . . tell me everything, even the things you aren't happy with (especially all the yucky stuff)

_____

_____

_____

_____

_____

_____

_____

_____

_____

_____

_____

_____

_____

- WHAT DO YOU SPEND MOST OF YOUR TIME THINKING ABOUT?

_____

_____

_____

_____

_____

_____

_____

Do you spend most of your time planning how you are going to make your life different or better than it is now?   YES____NO____

Do you spend most of your time wondering why you don't have the things you want now?   YES____NO____

Do you spend most of your time thinking how great your life would be if you could just figure out how to CREATE THE LIFE YOU DESIRE?   YES____NO____

If you answered "Yes" to ANY of the above questions, then congratulations! You HAVE been using the Law of Attraction . . . but you are attracting what you DON'T want instead of what you DO want. You may THINK you are doing the all the right things, and using the 5 steps of the Law of Attraction to work FOR you. Maybe you visualize and take time to Focus on what you desire every single day. But, if you answered "yes" to any of the above questions, chances are good that during the rest of the day, your mind gets ATTACHED to getting out of debt, or making more money, or losing more weight, or finding love or any other form of lack you have in your life—and THAT is EXACTLY what the Law of Attraction continues to bring you! If you go to a restaurant and order a steak and then realize you don't feel like having steak and you want the fish instead, do you sit there and talk about how disappointed your are feeling because you are going to have steak when you really wanted the fish—or do you simply take action and change your order? The answer is really simple—YOU CHANGE YOUR ORDER!

If you tune into a radio station day after day that plays music you hate, do you sit there complaining about the music and focusing on how much you wish you were listening to something different, or do you take action and get up and change the channel? YOU CHANGE THE CHANNEL! If you hate your job or home or life in any way, you probably spend a decent amount of time feeling like you have to accept it, wishing it wasn't what it is. I'm not going to pretend it's easy (I said using the Law is Attraction was SIMPLE, but rarely is it EASY!) But you CAN change your reality and all you have to do is literally change the channel and change your order. The good news is that because you are already using the Law of Attraction and the five steps of the Law of Attraction to create what you DON'T want, you can also use it to create what you DO want.

There's a struggle that many people experience—they know that the Law of Attraction is working, and they KNOW that they obviously have SOME blocks against attracting what they desire, but they can't figure out WHAT their blocks are. They honestly can't identify what they REALLY believe and focus on all day long. This is so because most of the time, you are unaware of the thoughts you are thinking at any given time throughout the course of a day. Your thoughts are like an underground river—you don't even know that its there—but it can certainly powerfully effect the manifestation of things that you desire in your life. We repeat the same thoughts over and over again, and this repetition becomes such a habit that our thoughts are actually attracting what we don't want on auto pilot.

ONE SMALL STEP: Identify What You DO Think About

So how do you discover what you're thinking about most of the time?

- Grab a pen, or open a new document on your computer, and set a timer for five minutes.

- DESCRIBE EXACTLY HOW YOUR LIFE IS RIGHT NOW. Don't be scared of judging it . . . go ahead and judge it . . . describe your life as you see it now, in great detail.

_____

_____

_____

_____

_____

_____

_____

_____

_____

- Access all of your senses and identify all that you currently see, feel, taste, sense, hear, touch, and smell in the description of your current life experience.

_____

_____

_____

_____

_____

_____

_____

- How does this make you FEEL? Limit your writing to five minutes only.

_____

_____

_____

_____

_____

_____

_____

_____

_____

_____

_____

_____

_____

_____

_____

_____

_____

_____

_____

_____

_____

_____

_____

_____

_____

_____

_____

_____

_____

_____

_____

_____

_____

_____

_____

OK, now that you're done, you probably aren't feeling your most upbeat and may even be questioning my sanity in giving you this exercise. I'll tell you why . . . I want you to get EXCITED and to feel GREAT about your life. I want you to wake up in the morning, excited about the life you are attracting each and every moment. But if I don't help you see what the Law of Attraction is bringing you right now, then you will never get to where you want to be. The point is, you have already harnessed the Law of Attraction. It is working every moment of every day. The only problem is that right now, you are attracting what you don't want. It's time for that to change . . . So let's dive into the Five steps in the Law of Attraction, and make them work FOR you instead of AGAINST you!

First, we need to identify what the Law of Attraction is bringing you now, and then we will turn that around so that you can start attracting what you DO want, instead of what you DON'T want. You have to be honest about what you're attracting to yourself now, even if it isn't what you want, and you need to accept that you are attracting it. I don't want you to blame yourself—blame is a waste of your precious heartbeats. But I do want you to take RESPONSIBILITY for it all, because when you do, you will realize that you already have all the power you need!

STEP ONE: Decide What You Want

What do you want? Be specific. Don't say "To be rich" or "To lose weight" or "To find my perfect soul mate" . . . those are just vague concepts without anything to define them.

- WHAT DO YOU WANT? Write it down now.

_____
_____
_____
_____
_____
_____
_____
_____
_____
_____
_____
_____
_____
_____
_____
_____
_____
_____

Great. Now let me ask you again . . .

- What is your life like right now? Be specific and write it all down.

_____
_____

_____

_____

_____

_____

_____

_____

_____

_____

_____

_____

_____

_____

What you have now is what your subconscious BELIEVES you want—and the only reason it thinks this is what you want is because you spend a lot more time thinking about what you DON'T want than what you DO want.

In fact, you are probably extremely clear about EXACTLY what it is you don't want, while you might only have a SENSE of what you DO want, and because of that, it isn't as clear in your mind.

The key point of the Law of Attraction is that whatever vision you hold is most clear, vivid and specific, WINS! That is what you will attract and create!

So what do you do now?

First we have to make what you DO WANT clearer and more defined. The more clear you are, the easier it will be for you to focus on and continually bring your attention back to what you DO want, especially when you are tempted to focus on what you don't want. We have clarified your order to the Universe by repeatedly asking those questions mentioned above (ie: "What do you want?") Note: The more details you can bring to mind about what you want, the better the result you will receive. If you can see, feel, touch, taste, smell and be blinded by the vivid color of your dream, then that's brilliant! Lose yourself in the details. That's what you want. Next I'll give you tools to get the new message to your subconscious mind, so it knows you have changed your order.

STEP TWO: Visualize In Great Detail

Take five minutes right now to Visualize yourself living the life you desire. I want you to really see yourself in this life.

- What do you SEE, HEAR, TASTE, SMELL and TOUCH? How do you FEEL?
- See it as if it is a movie; watch yourself participating FULLY in this life.
- Who are the people around you?
- What are you wearing?
- Where are you?
- What are you doing?

Watch this movie of yourself, and when it is completely clear in your mind, step INTO the body that is "you" in the movie, so that you literally go from watching it to LIVING it! How do you feel? Get excited, soak it in, notice every detail and KNOW that YOU DID THIS, you created this and you are living it now!

Take five minutes to do this exercise. If you really do this, you will feel pretty excited after it, but chances are that you also met with some RESISTANCE in your mind, and that's what we'll talk about in the next step . . .

STEP THREE: Remove Resistance To Your Dream

Here's the truth that you might not like . . . If you weren't somehow resisting what you want, you would already HAVE it. It's really THAT simple. So how do you REMOVE the resistance?

- <u>RELAX BEFORE YOU VISUALIZE:</u> If you are feeling stressed out and desperate and decide you need to visualize so you can get what you desire, how well do you think that's going to go? Do some deep breathing exercises before you visualize and then ALWAYS start by watching yourself like you're in a movie. Once you FEEL yourself enjoying the movie, that is the time to step INTO it—it is at that time that you are at your most receptive.

- <u>WRITE DOWN EVERY OBJECTION YOU HAVE TO WHAT YOU WANT:</u> Do you feel like it's too late to get what you want or that you aren't smart enough, or that you don't have enough connections, or that you'll have to make too many sacrifices to make money in your own business, lose all that weight etc? Write all your objections down, and get it out of your head. This is one of the best ways to diffuse the energy behind objections. The monster under the bed only gets bigger and bigger until you turn on the light! Once you've started clearing the obstacles, it's time for the next step . . .

- <u>DESCRIBE A TIME WHEN YOU EXPERIENCED SUCCESS:</u> It doesn't have to be a HUGE success. What did you have to BELIEVE to get that success? Why did it come to you? How were you different when it came to that success than you are in relation to your current goal? If you have been successful at anything, even in a small way, then you have within you the capability for great success, we just need to take that previous success and who you had to be to achieve that success, and connect it to what you want now.

STEP FOUR: Take Inspired Action

The Key to the Law of Attraction is Inspired Action! The Law of Attraction doesn't mean you sit around your house, visualizing what you want and then wait for it to knock on your door. This is the biggest misconception about the Law of Attraction, and definitely THE most dangerous one! The fact of the matter is that you could KNOW exactly what you want and you could be free of all your blocks, but if you don't listen to your intuition and take INSPIRED ACTION, chances are good that you will never get to your vision.

Put simply, if you try to take action BEFORE you go through the first two steps (Decide What You Want and Visualize Yourself Having It Already), I can almost guarantee that it won't be INSPIRED ACTION that you're taking. Inspired action comes from that gut instinct or sudden flash of an idea. Inspired action comes when you are clear about what you desire and are truly focused on what you DO want, instead of what you DON'T want. Inspired action is OFFENSIVE, not DEFENSIVE in nature. You know all of the answers somewhere inside you, it's just a matter of getting clear enough so that you can tap into that source. Start listening to yourself, and you'll start to tap into your "Inner Silent Partner" and all the wisdom you have. Once you do that, you're ready for the final step . . .

STEP FIVE: RELEASE YOUR ATTACHMENT

OK, now you're crystal clear on WHAT you want, you can visualize it in great detail, and actually FEEL how it feels to live the life you desire by stepping INTO that vision, and you are actively removing your blocks and connecting to your Inner Silent Partner to take inspired action . . . Now what? It's quite simple. And yet it's the hardest part of the equation . . .

You have to TRUST the Universe, TRUST the work you have done, COMMIT to keeping your focus on what you DO want and off what you DON'T want, and then . . . LET IT GO!

By all means, do things to keep your attention on what you want . . . put pictures up to anchor your mind on what you want . . . visualize it as if it is already your life now . . . and take INSPIRED ACTION.

But let go of the how and when it will come. Simply trust that it WILL come. The hardest part of attracting what you desire is letting go of the need to figure out HOW it will come to you. Let it go . . . and when your mind begs you to try to figure it out . . . let it go. If you try to figure it out, the only thing you will succeed in doing is to psych yourself out. Let go of how it will happen and know that what you want is already on its way to you and the Law of Attraction will work for you, instead of against you.

CHAPTER 9

RAISE YOUR VIBRATION

"Shoot for the moon. Even if you miss, you will land among the stars!"
~ Les Brown

Feelings are everything, they are the key when it comes to creating. Feelings will ATTRACT your desires to you and feelings will REPEL them away from you. Some feelings will SPEED your desires into your life and others will BLOCK your desires altogether. Abundance is your natural state. The way that you feel is your indicator of whether you are letting in the flow of abundance that is natural to you and always there for you—or whether you are pushing it away. If you are feeling expansive and light, then you will be able to attract the abundance you desire; if you feel constricted and heavy, then it will be an uphill battle. As I have said many times over, what you focus on is what you create. Rather than continually monitoring your thoughts and words, it is actually far easier if you FOCUS on the FEELINGS and ACTIONS that EXPAND your energy and RAISE your vibration. Start by doing things that make you feel good. When you feel good, you naturally begin thinking empowering thoughts and saying things that uplift you; you automatically become magnetic to your dreams. Life becomes easy; you get in the flow.

There are many benefits to being in a high vibrational state:

- You feel energized and radiant
- You feel supported, safe and secure.
- You become empowered

- You experience increased clarity and awareness.
- You feel alive and free
- You effortlessly achieve more balance in life.
- You take on a youthful glow and a childlike exuberance.
- Your health naturally improves
- You are confident and enthusiastic
- You experience improved health
- You experience synchronicity consistently
- You get in the flow and life becomes easy.
- You consistently think and feel empowered emotions

There are many ways to raise your energy, or vibration, but the most important is to honor yourself. The Universe will only look after you if you look after yourself. This means that if you think so lowly of yourself that you eat rubbish, take toxins into your body, are overweight, unorganized, stressed and living in chaos and you feel guilty about it all, then you are making a strong statement to the Universe. And that statement is that you don't think you're worth much—and that's exactly what you will attract back into your life—not much!

If you are feeling expansive and light, then you will be able to attract the Abundance you desire

So it makes sense to take excellent care of yourself. Your body is your temple—treat it as one. If you don't look after your body, where are you going to live? All those things you've heard about eating your vegetables, getting enough sleep, and drinking more water are more than a Pollyanna approach to feeling good—they are magical things that will increase your vibration and make you more attractive to prosperity, abundance and wealth! As you raise your vibration you get in the flow and things begin to happen easily and effortlessly. You experience synchronicity and meaningful coincidences.

Do these things to honor yourself every day and your energy or vibration will automatically rise:

- Spend quiet time each day in contemplation, prayer or meditation—whatever feels right to you.
- Learn to meditate, it is a powerful skill that will transform your life
- Exercise and look after your physical self—the better you feel physically, the higher vibration you will naturally be.
- Organize and beautify your surroundings—get rid of clutter and things you don't use. Turn off the TV and listen to uplifting music.
- Nourish your body with life-giving foods—as within, so without. The more alive and energized you are on the inside, the more you energetic you will be on the outside. Your world without—in every way—reflects the world within.
- Reduce toxins from your life—alcohol, cigarettes, sugar, and stress.
- Rest when you feel tired and get a peaceful night's sleep.
- Spend time with people who uplift, inspire and support you.
- Feed your mind with uplifting, inspiring and growth-oriented information—throw away the magazines and newspapers; read books that make you magnetic to prosperity and happiness and it will be yours.

Show the Universe that you value you. Once you value you more—you will find more will flow to you. Here are some more things to focus on that will expand your energy and raise your vibration:

- Feeling connected to and supported by the Universe
- Being enthusiastic
- Having massages
- Taking Inspired Action
- Being more loving
- Feeling grateful
- Laughing
- Feeling joy

- Praising others and accepting praise
- Any form of energy work
- Repeating empowering affirmations
- Creating a void through clearing clutter—in your house, car, cupboards etc
- Thinking uplifting and inspiring thoughts
- Accepting love
- Feeling deserving
- Spending time in nature
- Having fun
- Doing what you love
- Singing and dancing
- Playing silly games with your children or friends
- Listening to empowering CD's
- Watching empowering DVD's
- Cuddling your kids
- Spending time with positive friends
- Connecting to like-minded people through Mastermind groups etc
- Feeling the joy of being alive, being a creator, being the designer of your future and knowing that anything is possible!

When you raise your vibration and then apply the techniques suggested here, your results will appear so much faster than if you try and create from a low vibrational state. On a metaphysical level, it's difficult to take action when you are feeling heavy and your vibration is slow. Think of that statement from a purely physical perspective: If you were suddenly selected to run or walk a 500km Ultra marathon and would receive $1,000,000 just for finishing, I'm sure you'd attempt to do it. But more than likely it would be a long and arduous journey. You may even feel like giving up along the way. You might eventually get there, but it would probably take you 10 times longer than someone who was physically and psychologically prepared for such an arduous challenge.

Your world without—in every way—reflects your world within

Let's say on the other hand, you were not only eating well, exercising daily, getting plenty of sleep and generally looking after your 'temple', you were also training to run a marathon sometime in the future. If you had the same $1,000,000 challenge, you would jump at the chance with wild enthusiasm. And yes, it may be very challenging—but I bet you would get there a whole lot quicker. That's exactly how it works on the metaphysical plane. If you are 'training' for wealth by raising your vibration AND implementing the strategies mentioned here, you will find it comes a whole lot quicker! There is a definite connection between the Body, Mind, and Spirit trinity. One affects the other; it's all about balance. Nourish yourself physically, empower your mind and uplift your spirit. When you nurture all three, you will naturally energize your attracting powers! So open your arms to a life of Prosperity by loving yourself and your body—look after yourself, do what makes you happy and you will see the abundance flood into your life!

> "To believe in the things you can see and touch is no belief at all,
> but to believe in the unseen is a triumph and a blessing."
> ~Abraham Lincoln ~

If you are applying all you learn, but not yet seeing any increased prosperity in your life, you may be missing an important piece of the puzzle. There is a crucial point in getting rich where thought and personal action must be combined. There are many people who, consciously or subconsciously, set the creative forces in action (placing their order with the Universe) by the strength and persistence of their desires, but who remain poor because they are not prepared to receive that which they desire. This concept was first discussed in 'The Science of Getting Rich' by Wallace Wattles.

> "By thought, the thing you want is brought to you.
> By action, your receive it!"
> ~ Wallace Wattles ~

This is VITAL information, so critical, and I often repeat it because it is so crucial to really absorb these words. If you have struggled with money all your life, or maybe you've just got by but never really got ahead (whatever that means) then I liken the energy you have in relation to money similar to an invisible force field surrounding you. You can do all the affirmations, visualizations, goal setting and thinking in the world, but when you do attract your desires and they get within 'spitting distance' of you, they can't get through your force field. They simply do not appear in your world because you do not have an opening for them to enter. There is thought and there is action. You can get out there and do, do, do all day long. But unless your mind is open to receiving wealth, your results will be minimal. You can also go and perch yourself on a mountain top and meditate all day long, willing wealth to drop in your lap, but again, unless you take some action—as they say, "It ain't gonna happen!" You HAVE to marry the two; you MUST combine the metaphysical (thinking and feeling) with practical action.

I like the story about the man who decided he was going to win the lottery. He wrote down his goal and chanted it daily. He spent time in quiet meditation, reflecting on the joy of winning his millions and visualized himself joyously spending all that cash. The days, which soon turned into weeks, passed and still no big lottery win. Things started to get desperate; he was way behind in his rent and then received notice they were coming to repossess his car. In a panic he ran out into the back yard, looked up to the heavens, threw his hands up in frustration and yelled "Lord, you know things have not been going well with my business. I could really use this money. I don't understand. I have been diligently meditating, I've been praying, I've been picturing my big win and saying my affirmations every single day. I'm doing everything possible but the money isn't here yet. What more could I possibly do?" A voice boomed down from the Heavens and said "Meet me halfway . . . buy a ticket!"

I love this little story, because it clearly illustrates the difference between thought and action. The Universe simply cannot deliver if you do not take action. This could be the reason why YOU are not receiving the abundance you have ordered.

"The way the Universe works is quite simple—
you have a desire and it is always answered, every single time."
~ Abraham-Hicks ~

There are only three points to the fulfillment of your wishes, goals and dreams.

- The CREATION, or the asking. That one's easy; it comes naturally—it is what you desire. You really don't have to work on that one at all; it just appears out of nowhere! In the moment you think of what it is you desire, you are asking for that desire.
- The ANSWERING TO THAT ASKING: That is when the Universe, or God, or Spirit, always gives the answer or 'your order' in the moment you are asking. As I mentioned before, you only have that desire because it's in your warehouse, so the Universe has already provided it. It has answered your call; your desire is on its way.
- RECEIVING WHAT YOU'VE ASKED FOR: If there's something that you have been waiting for that is not yet manifesting in your experience, it isn't because of point one (the asking) or point two (the answering) it can only be that you are not in the receiving mode.

So to receive you must take action. You must have an unwavering belief that your desire will appear and you must be grateful (acting as if it has ALREADY appeared).

ONE SMALL STEP: Set Your Action Plan

- Believe, take action and be grateful.
- Write down 3 actions you can take NOW to move you toward your desire (and take those actions TODAY!)

1. _____
2. _____
3. _____

If your greatest desire is to be rich, but you are not rich now, then you are going to be in a constant state of tension, because you are stretching and moving out of your comfort zone—the only way to relax in that state of tension is to feel it often enough that you get used to it; in other words, practice the strategies suggested here daily.

If you were unfit and decided to run a marathon, but only trained really hard once a week, and the rest of the time you sat around and ate junk food—you would always be sore, always in pain, and you'd never run that marathon. It's the same with being rich. If you focus on being rich and think about it once a week, and the rest of the time focus on your debts and money problems, you will remain in a state of tension most of the time, and you will never achieve the riches you desire. You must 'train' daily; think about wealth, picture wealth, dream of all you will do with your wealth. Do it daily. And you WILL be rich! If you persist, then your world will change. As with anything new, it can sometimes seem like too much effort (and we usually want perfect results yesterday!) You will have to remember to make time for and PRACTICE your strategies and exercises. It may even seem like a chore—but you can choose NOT to think of it that way!!! The second you have that negative, clingy feeling, you're losing energy, giving away your power, effectively lowering your vibration, and you begin to attract from a place of lack.

Day by day, as you repeat the various strategies explained here, you will enjoy them more and more, you will embrace them, they will become part of who you are and then you will do them automatically. You will begin to see evidence that you have tapped into that great river of Abundance. Then life becomes a joy. You are in the flow and you will be a money magnet!

*"We all know that a rocket burns most of its fuel
during the first few moments of flight as it overcomes inertia
and the gravitational pull of the earth.
That's what it's like for us as we launch our dreams into physical reality."*
~Maria Nemeth ~

The road to a life filled with abundance can often be a rocky one with many twists and turns. Sometimes it can seem easier to stay where you are, deep within your comfort zone, than it is to venture out into uncharted territory, where you could live the life of your dreams. You may experience the ups and downs when it comes to money. You may create wealth, only to lose it. You may tap into the flow of abundance, only to see it dry up once again. Don't despair. Just KNOW that the prosperity you desire is ALWAYS there. Your riches are always waiting for you, always surrounding you. Sometimes the cash isn't there because you are still expanding your comfort zone around money and on a subconscious level, you push away the money that is beyond what you are used to. And sometimes the money isn't there because you choose to think it's not coming. But please remember, what you think, what you believe, and what you speak is what you end up creating. I have learnt a valuable lesson. Sometimes life does not go the way you planned. Full stop. End of lesson. The thing is, when it doesn't go the way you would have preferred, you have two choices. One is to go with the flow, accept it, and move on. The other is to get annoyed, feel angry, rant and rave about how unfair it is and focus on it so much that you re-create it again and again in your life.

Are you re-creating challenges, dramas and bad luck over and over in your life by focusing on it, thinking about it, analyzing it, phoning your friends and telling them about it? Let it go and move on! Re-create a new and empowered future by letting go of the past—today! You have to face the responsibility of where you are in your life right now. You can no longer blame your past, your present or your future, your family, your friends, your job, your boss, the economy, your age, your weight, your knowledge, your location, your health or anything else in the entire world!

Everything that has occurred in your life is because YOU thought it first, maybe consciously, maybe subconsciously. Maybe you were just focusing so much on what you didn't want, that you attracted it right into your life. It doesn't matter any longer. You KNOW the secret to living the life of your dreams now, so go live it!

Keep your focus on what you DO WANT, and then persist!
Don't ever give up, matter what happens . . . and it will be yours!

When you begin to tap into your wealth, when it begins to flow to you and then, for whatever reason it disappears, don't focus on how you don't have it any more, focus on how you did have it, and how that is evidence that you already know how to attract wealth. Focus on how much fun it was, even if it was a brief moment, (and even if it was only a tiny piece of prosperity) and you will surely attract even more to you, because the Universe can hardly wait to give you all you desire and then some!

Also don't get stuck in the twilight zone—where you think about what you desire half the time, and what you don't want the other half. If you think about prosperity and riches and wealth, and then worry about how you will pay your bills—the Universe cannot be clear about exactly what to send you, so you may get a little of both, (a bit of money coming in, then more bills coming in) or you may get more of one than the other; a little bit of money and a LOT of bills—especially it you worry MORE about your debts than feeling excited about being rich!

Everything in your world is there because you thought of it, so if you change your thoughts to that of total prosperity, abundance, wealth and riches ALL the time, it has been scientifically proven that you WILL begin to experience total prosperity, abundance, wealth and riches ALL THE TIME!!! It has to happen; there can be no other outcome! This is science based on Universal Law, and if one person gets rich from it, then it is a fact that YOU too can get rich.

*"Desire is God tapping at the door of your mind,
trying to give you greater good. That you deeply desire something is
positive proof that it has already been prepared for you,
and is only waiting for you to recognize and accept it."*
~ Catherine Ponder ~

As we go through our days measuring ourselves against an infinite landscape of yardsticks, our panic button gets hit again and again. The brain, in order to help us escape all these threats sends signals to the body to release adrenalin and cortisol, the hormones designed to save us from being eaten by lions. As you might imagine, they're potent and powerful chemicals. Pumping them into the system regularly not only damages the body by also changes it, making it easier and easier to turn on the stress response. "If I'm in this much danger" the brain thinks, "I'd better open up the channels a little bit." And soon you're operating at a hopped-up level well above where you should be, struggling with sleep problems, feeling fatigued, and having almost completely forgotten how to have fun. Your cells have forgotten too. When your cells receive these hormonal signals, they change their configuration. They stop their happy labour and start conserving energy. If your immune system is in the middle of fighting an infection, it stops, because all of the body's energy is being diverted to saving your ass from the huge threat looming on the horizon. And we wonder why our gums bleed and our wounds won't heal and our allergies kick up. There's only so much energy in the system, and as a result, it's impossible for the body to support both the growth mode and the protection mode at the same time.

Given that your goal is now to amplify your dream life into reality, where will you get the energy for that? It's clear that when your body is in protection mode, it will not be able to support your creation process in an optimum way, or even at all. So the trick is to keep your body in growth mode and then stoke the system to produce maximum energy.

The triggers that cause your body to produce a stress response are purely the result of your perception of them as a threat. We have beliefs about who we are and how the world works. Some of these beliefs are factual, and some of them are based on information we've received during our lifetimes that it not true.

ACTIVITIES TO RAISE YOUR VIBRATIONAL SET POINT:

OK let's go swimming! We want to drench ourselves in the belief that our vision is coming true. Like a raft floating in a pool, your beliefs can buoy you up. Like a rubber ducky, they can make you lighten up and laugh. Like playing with toy boats, practicing your beliefs can take your mind off your worries and help you refocus on your amplification process. Like a good bubble bath, your beliefs can calm you and reconnect you to your purpose. So lets look at some of the "toys" that are available for you to turbo charge your beliefs.

- MEDITATION: can literally change the way your brain is wired for action. Don't you think it would be a good idea to spend some time training your brain to generate the emotions you want to feel, to focus on the images you want to create, and to release the thoughts that no longer serve you? Even a little dose of meditation might be able to help.
- CONTEMPLATION AND REFLECTION: Spend regular time sitting with your thoughts about your dreams and the goals you want to achieve. How can you expect to gain new knowledge and insight, if you are always moving too fast and talking too loudly to hear what your Higher Self has to suggest.
- VISUALIZATION: Creating a list of the things you want to visualize and assigning each thing to a day of the week, might be one way to organize your visualization habit. Identify some specific milestone events that will be indicators that your dream life is coming true. Can you see each one?

- IMMERSIVE PROBLEM SOLVING: Do you believe you can do it? Then just DO IT! Want to be the top salesperson in your company? Make those cold calls. Need to get folks to sponsor your bike trip across Italy? Set up that website. Want to buy a house on the water? Pick up real estate magazines and start visiting open homes. Nothing convinces your brain more than when you become actively involved in making your dream come true, as long as your actions are aligned to your beliefs.
- THE IMAGINED AUDIENCE: Tell the story of your success to an imaginary audience. By putting your passion into words, you'll find yourself becoming more and more clear about what you want to create. It will begin to feel as if it's already a fait accompli. Imagine that you've been asked to give the commencement speech at a university. What will you tell your audience about what you've created in life? What keys to success will you pass on? You might also pretend to have a conversation with an old friend you haven't seen in a while, and imagine her amazement at how you've changed your life. Your confident report on the future will make you feel more confident about your amplification process in the present.
- BLOGGING: You can share the process of amplifying your dream into reality by posting your progress online. Your collected posts will become a public journal of your success.
- VLOGGING: The cool thing about vlogging (creating a video log and posting it online) is that you will capture moments when you are in a positive productive state, and at other moments when you are not so positive! Study the differences between the two. What inspired you to get so psyched up one day and not on another? Did something specific happen? Did you wake up with excited, supportive thoughts in your head? Once you identify your positive triggers, then you can be empowered to activate them when you need to.
- JOURNALLING: Write down your observations about your beliefs and about how your beliefs influence your

behavior. This is about creating awareness, and recording the discoveries you make while being aware. Write down the reasons why you are destined to create your dream. If you're distracted, a journal is a great place to dump all the thoughts spinning you around, so that you get them out of your head and recorded on paper, and then get back on the right track toward your dream.

- PRE-THANKING: Lastly, you can thank the Universe in advance, as if your dream creation has already come true. Pre-thanking is a great way to remind yourself of how you will feel once your vision has become reality, because it forces you to be mentally in the place where it's already happened. By managing and nurturing your beliefs, you will create the right kind of internal environment, one that will keep you in growth mode and maximize the use of your energy.

SELF PROGRAMMING FOR SUCCESS:

A self-empowered person views success as a constant companion.

STEP 1: IDENTIFY YOUR GOAL OF SUCCESS: What does success mean to you? How does it relate to your sense of self, to your education and training, to your dreams of completeness and fulfillment, and so forth? The important difference here between specific goal identification and your goal of success is that Success is the Big Picture. It's not just becoming the President-Elect of the United States, but your vision of you as the historical figure of the President for the next four or eight years, and what you expect to accomplish and how you will be seen.

At the same time that this is your big picture of success, it doesn't mean that all else is excluded. Condoleezza Rice was not only Secretary of State but she was also a respected concert pianist. Hilary Clinton not only became Secretary of State but she remained a wife and mother. The big picture is inclusive of your major success but also all other important parts of your life related to that success. Success is who you are in the outer world.

STEP 2: WRITE IT DOWN: Always write your success picture down. Review it from time to time, change it as time goes by to reflect the changes in your life but still remembering the successful person you are. And as those changes occurred you may have a second successful career. Success is evolutionary because you are always evolving. You are never just one thing, but your big picture should represent the success of who you are now.

STEP 3: ANALYZE THE CHALLENGES: There is always a challenge, no matter who you are and where you are. Even at the peak of your success, there are challenges and your analysis of the big picture must recognize those challenges and how you will successfully meet them. It's not the details of HOW you become the President who will win the War on Terrorism, but how you will see yourself as the President who successfully won the War of Terror (ie: WHO you will be).

STEP 4: WRITE DOWN YOUR EXPECTATIONS: Always write it down. It is essential to bring the inner vision into your outer reality, and the first step in this process is to write it down in your journal. And then review your journal entries to bring that vision back inside yourself and modify it as things progress. The final phase it to externalize the modified vision by recording it in your journal too.

STEP 5: WRITE AN "I AM" SENTENCE: When dealing with the Big Picture of your success, remember to keep it flexible and evolutionary. For example: "I am successfully fulfilling my job as a great defense attorney" is an affirmation that allows you to move within the boundaries of statement. It is important not to confuse your big picture goals with the many individual goals that will be part of your life every day. Your success as a great defense attorney is not a function of your weight loss program, which may be represented in the sentence "I AM slim." The big picture is more than the sum of those little pictures we discussed previously as goals.

STEP 6: MEMORIZE YOUR "I AM" SENTENCE: And practice it many times throughout the day, really getting into the feeling of the situation being true.

STEP 7: VISUALIZE IT: Close your eyes and visualize the sentence in White Letters against a black background. As you see it, speak the sentence with your inner voice.

STEP 8: CREATE AN IMAGE OR SYMBOL: Now silently ask your subconscious mind to produce a simple image or symbol to fully represent that sentence. This is the symbol of your success. This is your 'talisman' of success. It's like a very personal and very real "good luck charm." Your subconscious mind has called out to the collective unconscious to find a powerful symbol of your success. Memorize it, and draw it—no matter what your artistic skills are (this helps to engrave it into your subconscious mind).

STEP 9: MEMORIZE IT: See your image or symbol in the same mental scene as your "I AM" sentence. Know that you now have the power to make your dream come true.

STEP 10: THE NEW REALITY: Remember that you are leaving an old reality behind and replacing it with a new reality that is you as your 'Successful Self'. See yourself in this new reality as if it has already happened. Make this your future NOW. Feel yourself in the new reality, repeat your vision of the image and your "I AM" sentence together, and hear your inner voice say it. Tie it all together so any time you repeat the sentence in your mind, you know that what is accomplished in the Inner World is manifesting in the physical world, and that your body, mind and spirit are working together to bring this about.

You are a self-empowered person and success is your constant companion. Success in not just a momentary, fleeting experience, but is an ongoing process of you always meeting your individually stated goals. All those accomplished goals are like beads strung on a necklace that is as intrinsic to your self-image as it is your badge of office. You must have a clear mental picture of the correct action you need to take, BEFORE you can complete it. And you need a still mind to contemplate such an action, hence it is important to clearly picture the end result.

If you lack confidence in your ideas and abilities, you will often ask the opinion of others. This opens you to the possibility of disappointment, when the opinions of others are mostly negative. It is preferable and more constructive to listen to your inner voice. If you do this with awareness, that inner voice will guide you on the right path. You might want to ask the opinion of others and if you do, whether they are positive or negative, simply beam your white light onto that person and listen. Bear in mind that no other person can tell you the answer that is relevant to you. Your wealth of knowledge comes from within. The opinions of others will be based on their experience, their view of the world.

REFERENCES

- 'Ask and It Is Given—Learning to Manifest the Law of Attraction' by Esther and Jerry Hicks. Hay House Inc. Carlsbad, USA. 2005.

- "Brain/Mind Bulletin", March 1980 by Charles Garfield

- 'Illusions' by Richard Bach. Bantam Doubleday Dell Publishing Group, New York, USA. 1994.

- 'Making It Happen: Reflections on Leadership' by Sir John Harvey-Jones. Profile Books, London. 2003.

- 'The Body of Life: Creating New Pathways for Sensory Awareness' by Thomas Hanna. Inner Traditions—Healing Arts Press, Rochester, VT, USA. 2000.

- 'The Inner Game of Tennis: The Classic Guide to the Mental Side of Peak Performance' by W. Timothy Gallwey. Random House T rade Paperbacks, New York, 2008.

- 'The Luck Factor: The Scientific Study of the Lucky Mind' by Professor Richard Wiseman,Arrow Books, UK. 2004.